BUDDHISM
FOR

Break-ups

BUDDHISM
FOR
Break-ups

MESHEL LAURIE

NERO

Published by Nero,
an imprint of Schwartz Publishing Pty Ltd
Level 1, 221 Drummond Street
Carlton VIC 3053, Australia
enquiries@blackincbooks.com
www.nerobooks.com

National Library of Australia Cataloguing-in-Publication entry (pbk)

Laurie, Meshel, author.
Buddhism for break-ups/ Meshel Laurie.
9781863959001 (paperback)
9781925435443 (ebook)
Buddhist philosophy.
Marital conflict—Religious aspects—Buddhism.
Interpersonal relations—Religious aspects—Buddhism.
Self-actualization (Psychology)—Religious aspects—Buddhism.

Cover design by Peter Long
Photo by Elizabeth Allnutt
Back cover illustration by Silverlane
Text design and typesetting by Tristan Main

Printed in Australia by McPherson's Printing Group.

FSC
www.fsc.org
MIX
Paper from
responsible sources
FSC® C001695

Contents

Introduction

My Story

When my marriage was ending, I desperately searched for a Buddhist book about break-ups, but I couldn't find a single one. Maybe it's because monks and nuns are celibate. I once heard someone ask His Holiness the 14th Dalai Lama if he ever regretted not being married or having a family. He replied that if he ever finds himself thinking that way, he just talks to his married friends. Then he started chuckling, and his eyes sparkled mischievously as he added, 'Soon I'm thinking celibacy is better for peaceful life!'

I started pulling together bits and pieces myself from lots of different Buddhist sources, and quickly discovered that break-ups are an excellent prism through which to study Buddhist principles, because they highlight so many of our human fears and frailties. No matter how unique we think we are, a broken heart challenges us all in very similar ways, ways that tend to be closely linked to our most primitive selves. Buddha realised that these issues and the ways we cope with them are the foundation of our emotional lives. They determine how happy we are. He developed a road map for gaining control, so that we can *create* happiness, rather than just stumble around hoping to randomly run into it.

Let's face it: we're still pretty primitive beings in a lot of ways. Until someone develops an app that makes us relaxed and happy no matter what's going on around us (drug-free and with no comedown), Buddha's step-by-step ancient self-help program is about as simple and effective a model as you'll ever come across. It's perfect for our modern lives – and you won't need to buy any machines or exotic fruits for this spiritual detox. Just read through these principles and allow yourself some quiet time to think about them. All you have to do is take the leap and face yourself.

Let me explain how I came to do that.

No matter how good they look, someone, somewhere is sick of their shit.

That's my all-time favourite piece of graffiti wisdom. It was written very high up on a wall in the sticky back room of a pub where I performed stand-up gigs at least once a week in my early twenties. I don't know who said it first, but I'm pretty sure it wasn't Buddha (although I dare say he'd agree with the sentiment).

In those days, when I wasn't gigging at pubs I was spending my time falling in love with Adrian. Tall, slim and classically handsome, with thick brown hair, full pouting lips, high cheekbones and big blue eyes, Adrian definitely looked good. And, sure enough, he told me straight away that there were a few ladies around the traps who were well and truly sick of his shit (as well as handsome, Adrian is unfailingly honest and self-deprecating – what a package, huh?).

But I refused to believe I'd ever be sick of anything about this lovely man – who somehow managed to pull off sexy and goofy, straightforward and shy, sensible and artistically dreamy all at the same time. I jumped in with both feet and married him, six months to the day after we met on the smoker's landing at a compulsory work-for-the-dole program. (As you can see, the omens were fabulous!)

Not long before the wedding, I ceased a friendship with someone when I heard she'd made a nasty comment about us. 'Meshel's only marrying Adrian because he's the first man who's ever said he loves her,' this woman was reported to have said. How rude!

But how true. At twenty-three, I'd never had a boyfriend before. A few friends with benefits, sure. The odd accommodating stranger? Of course. But no-one to call my own. No-one who told me they loved me. You might not be surprised to find out that I had a difficult relationship with my father in my teens and early twenties. Now Adrian's love meant everything to me, and I was determined to hold onto it with everything I had.

I didn't want to listen to anyone's misgivings about our rush to the alter. At that stage in my life I was a big fan of avoiding unpleasant feelings whenever possible, by whatever means necessary. In fact, I was using heroin when Adrian and I first met. Luckily for me, he didn't like the idea and Adrian's attention comforted and numbed my pain so much that I stopped using. The fact that he was attracted to me was intoxicating.

His love was the best drug I'd ever tried. It blocked out every bad thing that had ever happened or which I feared was possible. Adrian's desire to be with me made me feel, for the first time since early childhood, that I had a place in the world.

Of course I wondered what on earth this wonderful being saw in me. When I asked him, he'd mutter, 'I don't know ... You're just ... nice,' or something equally profound.

On one memorable occasion, when asked what he was thinking, Adrian replied dreamily, 'Oh, I'm just thinking about smiles.'

I literally wept with joy at finding myself on a mattress on the floor of a dingy share house in Brunswick with such an ethereal poet.

(Eventually he felt guilty about my emotional reaction and admitted that 'Smiles' was the name of the souvlaki shop around the corner. Turned out he was just hungry.)

I wept with joy a lot in those early days. I couldn't believe he wanted to be with me. Looking back now, I think my biggest appeal for Adrian was that I offered him an *idea* of a future. He admits he was pretty lost at that point in time, and I probably looked as though I was going somewhere because I was very ambitious. When you're heading nowhere, someone else's *somewhere* can look pretty comforting.

In contrast to Adrian's share house, I lived by myself in a nice flat in St Kilda. Our respective dwellings were symbolic of our different approaches to life. I have always been driven to go out and make stuff happen, whereas Adrian often feels overwhelmed and exhausted from dealing with what life throws at him. The more time he can spend hiding from the world, the happier he is. Although neither of us had a lot of money, I had a knack of juggling and hustling which meant I had a pretty comfortable lifestyle. I lived in a cool suburb. I had a car. I went out for beers with my friends. I felt good about my life! In comparison, Adrian lived in a dump, with jerks, and felt like a loser. Paying for my lifestyle was a constant challenge, but I accepted it, while Adrian liked to keep his challenges to a minimum – and his creature comforts reflected this.

But despite these differences, like most couples, we found a way to coexist. We became a team. After my third or fourth sleepover at Adrian's place, stepping carefully over the gaping hole in the bathroom floor and creeping outside at night to the toilet (in inner suburban Melbourne in 1996), I proposed we base ourselves at my place. Thus began nineteen years of cohabitation. I didn't realise it at the time, but I was signing an unwritten agreement that would eventually hang like a weight around my neck. I became the president, vice-president and only staff member of the juggling and hustling department of our relationship. Our comfort – or, more specifically, paying for it – became my responsibility, and Adrian was never shy when it came to adding requirements for me to fulfil. I spent many sleepless nights wondering how I was going to pay our rent or mortgage, which worried Adrian not one jot! Not his department.

Before you become too outraged, I should explain that Adrian also took on a rather challenging portfolio in our relationship too. He became the boss of my self-worth, which I decided was entirely his to cultivate and maintain. For a very long time I treated every emotional wobble or crisis in confidence I had as his responsibility. I completely stopped contributing to my own emotional growth.

The two departments worked something like this: I'd sign a lease – or, later, a mortgage – agreeing to pay more money than I could afford so that we could live somewhere Adrian liked, and in return he'd provide the attention and affection I needed to approach the world with the confidence it took to find the money we needed.

For a long time this arrangement worked. I took great pride in making miracles happen and impressing

Adrian – and in turn he showered me with attention and affection. Over time, though, arrangements like this – where each partner takes on a fixed role in the relationship – often begin to chafe. We grow tired and yearn for a break from the responsibilities we've signed up for, but typically lack the self-awareness to ask for this in clear and loving ways. We generally just crack the shits more often.

But in the early days, I saw no chafing on the horizon. I was far too busy 'love-bombing' Adrian to consider we might be falling into bad habits. Love-bombing is a technique that psychopaths and cult leaders use, so I'm not particularly proud of it, although I didn't know that's what I was doing at the time. It basically means coming on very strong with flattery and affection. You make the object of your affection feel like someone finally appreciates their true worth, so it works particularly well on people with low self-esteem. As well as being on work-for-the-dole, Adrian was a country kid from a fractured family with a bad break-up in his past. He was ripe for love-bombing. I made him feel special and protected. I think he clung to me partly out of relief.

For many years, our relationship worked. We compensated for each other's weaknesses and formed a tight union of trust and support. We recognised that we were each quirky in our own way, and felt lucky to have a relationship in which we felt safe – me to throw caution to the wind and push my ambitious self out into the world, and Adrian to live a quiet life outside mainstream society, which terrifies him.

Adrian followed me around the country as I moved up the ranks of the entertainment industry. We'd often be given very short notice that we needed to move interstate. Adrian would worry and start packing, and I would reassure him the change would be positive. When we arrived at our new home, he'd worry and unpack, and I'd bury myself in my new job, throwing him a few reassuring words over my shoulder as I rushed out the door. It was like an inverted '60s sitcom: I was Darren from *Bewitched*, and he was the lovely Samantha. I was stressed, self-important and emotionally volatile, and he was serene – never expressing stresses or worries of his own. I tried to keep money worries to myself, and I showed my appreciation of Adrian by showering us in *things*, from Xboxes to overseas trips.

For most of my adult life, I've been sure that Adrian and I would never break up. Our relationship was the one thing I didn't have to worry about.

But I was wrong.

Adrian outgrew the dynamic we shared. He got tired of living in my shadow, as many spouses of go-getters do eventually. He wanted to seek his own identity.

I never stopped loving Adrian, but as he started to reject me, it stirred up lots of negative emotions that made it difficult for me to express my love. My ego told me he had no right to stop loving me after everything I'd done for him, and my fear told me I had to make him stay whether he liked it or not.

Whenever I allowed myself to consider my future post-break-up, I was paralysed by fear. I was afraid of being alone, afraid of him 're-partnering' – as the family lawyers put it – and afraid of dating. Just quietly, I was almost as terrified of having sex with someone else as I was of never having sex again. There's a lot to be afraid of out there!

Fortunately, I had somewhere to turn: Buddhism.

I first started studying Buddhism years earlier when I needed help dealing with work-related stress. Adrian had told me he was fatigued by the situation and sick of my moodiness. I was in a deep depression at the time, having lost a job I cherished. So I took myself off to classes at the nearest Buddhist centre once a week. They really helped and gave me a new perspective on life. As soon as I felt better, I stopped going regularly, but I would return occasionally whenever the going got rough.

Despite this, it took me a long time to fully embrace Buddhism as a solution when my marriage was floundering. I resisted it because I knew the first thing Buddhism would require me to do was to let go of Adrian – and that was the last thing in the world I wanted to do!

Eventually, though, I knew I had no option – *he* had let go of *me* and it was affecting every aspect of my life. At the time, I was doing a national drive-time radio show with Marty Sheargold and Tim Blackwell which was supposed to give people a laugh on their way home from work, and yet there I was, crying in my car for hours before every show. Fortunately, Tim and Marty are both brilliant, so my lack of input went unnoticed by everyone but me. You can get really lucky in this crazy business sometimes! But still: I needed help.

I've borrowed an expression from Alcoholics Anonymous to describe the way I use Buddhism in my life – 'working the program'. Instead of trying to figure out ways of coping with their addiction, members of AA focus on the clear roadmap of the Twelve Steps, committing themselves to just one of those steps at a time. Our marriage counsellor, James, joked with us once that Adrian and I are very creative people and we try some pretty creative ways to deal with problems. I faced the fact that I needed to stop being creative and start working the program as taught by Buddha over two and a half thousand years ago. I needed to surrender myself to his wisdom and to the wisdom of the great Buddhist scholars alive today. I had to have the humility to accept that I didn't have any answers. I had to *give up*.

At the heart of my stubbornness and the fears that went with it was the very simple fear of unhappiness. Like most humans, I had convinced myself that there was a long list of things I needed in order to be happy – and high on that list was a perfect partner: a soulmate, if you will. I believed I had found that in Adrian, and that therefore our relationship would last forever, but the fact is I was *always* bound to lose it, one way or another.

Take a minute to process that, because it's friggin' huge!

No relationship lasts forever. Even if Adrian and I had remained happily married for the rest of our lives, what are the chances of us dying at the same moment? It was always far more likely that one of us would have to face the loss of the other. And that's the case with any love affair – but it's not something most of us really want to think about, is it?

> All that live must surely die, and all that meet must part.
>
> BUDDHA

No relationship – romantic, familial or platonic – is absolute and forever. We will all lose someone we rely on at some point in our lives. Sometimes the other person chooses to leave us, sometimes they're taken from us tragically, and sometimes we discover they were never ours to begin with. But one way or another, the relationship will end. We know this is true, and yet we convince ourselves that our happiness depends on how other people see us, on how close they hold us, and on how faithfully they forsake others in our favour.

In the end, I was the one who initiated our divorce. Thanks to his fear of change, I'm sure Adrian would have stayed married to me. We could all have gone on pretending there was nothing unusual about the fact he lived in a granny flat out the back and didn't come anywhere near me when the kids weren't around. But there's no loneliness in the world like the loneliness of a loveless relationship.

No pillow talk, no sharing of TV shows, no in-jokes, no best friend to curl up with at the end of the day ... being married to someone who doesn't want to spend time with you is ... gosh, I can't even think of a word to describe it. No word encapsulates the rejection, disappointment and loneliness I felt, lying in bed alone, night after night, for years.

About five years to be more specific – that's how long it took me to learn that there's a fine line between commitment to a relationship and hitting your head against a brick wall.

Know well what leads you forward and what holds you back, and choose the path that leads to wisdom.

BUDDHA

In the months following our decision to divorce, whenever I started to wonder if I'd done the right thing, I was sent a sign.

One morning, for instance, I had an appointment for a haircut at our local shops. Adrian was heading out at the same time, so I asked him to give me a lift. It was sheer laziness on my part, as the shops are less than a ten-minute walk from our house.

Less than a ten-minute walk, but a fifteen-minute drive when Adrian is at the wheel. I knew I was in trouble when he turned right on leaving our driveway. The main street of our suburb is decidedly left of our driveway. Left and left again, to be exact – but not in Adrian's mind. In his mind, it's a right, then a left, then a traversing of the circumference of the entire neighbourhood until he happens back upon the main street. Then he passed eight empty parking spaces (yes, I was counting!) on his way to the furthest reach of the street, so that he could park where he always parks, in a quiet little off-street lot by the beach. Sitting in the passenger seat, incredulous, I was without exaggeration roughly the same distance from the hairdresser's as I had been sitting at home, only in the opposite direction.

By this stage running late, I delivered a short, sharp, expletive-ridden review of the journey before slamming the door and stomping off for my appointment. No doubt he was left wondering – as I was – how we managed to live together for so long. Adrian is a methodical, slow man of habit who likes to focus on one thing at a time, and I am a quick-witted multitasker with a glove box full of parking and speeding fines, who always believes she can fit in one more thing and fears nothing more than an unproductive moment.

A hairdressing salon is a great place to work off a bad mood. Particularly the one I frequent, which is very old-fashioned. Most of the women having their hair done that day had grown up in our suburb and were now in their seventies and eighties. They were shocked by a number of aspects of my story. Adrian's terrible navigational instincts came in for a serve, but so too did my lack of patience. Most troubling for the peanut gallery, though, was the news that we were in the process of divorcing after almost twenty years together, even though neither of us had committed a huge, relationship-exploding sin.

All the ladies in attendance, without exception, had been dropped off by their husbands. Two of those husbands were sitting on a bus seat outside the hairdresser's ready to take them home again. But the women assured me their relationships hadn't always been so close. One of the sweet old codgers sunning himself outside received a particularly eyebrow-raising character reference. His youthful wildness had been the stuff of legend around town and his poor wife had spent many a tearful night at home with a tribe of kids, wondering where he was, who he was with, when he'd be home and how much of her housekeeping money he'd squandered.

'Did you ever consider leaving him?' I asked.

'Ooh no,' she said, 'we didn't think like that in those days.'

In the process of deciding to divorce, I thought long and hard about what a marriage is and how it evolves. My marriage to Adrian had been passionate when it was supposed to be passionate, and for a long time it had been supportive when it needed to be supportive. If we toughed out this period of annoyance and squabbling, would we emerge into gentle old-age companionship? Would I end up with a sweet old man who held my handbag while I had my hair done? Or would I spend the next forty years tearing my hair out?

And then I challenged myself to think about things from a different perspective: a Buddhist perspective.

What if I accepted that I had no way of knowing what the future held?

What if I stopped worrying about the future and focused on the here and now?

What if I dealt calmly with my situation as it was, rather than as I wished it could be or feared it might become?

I realised that so much of my daily discord came down to arguing about things that hadn't happened yet. I was equally intense about what I *did* and *didn't* want to have happen, and ready to blame Adrian for everything. I can be a real barrel of laughs, let me tell you!

The Buddhist perspective tells me there are two big problems with this approach:

1. Future thinking.
2. Thinking someone else is responsible for my emotions.

Both of these have been lifelong problems for me. I've always loved forward planning – which at first sounds reasonable, but can very easily tip over into unnecessary worry. When that worry turns into arguing with a spouse over possible future events that they've never thought of, let alone developed a strategy for, it's potentially a big problem. And let's face it, modern life has enough real pressures without piling on panic attacks about fantasies!

As far as responsibility for my emotions goes, I know I'm not alone in sometimes saying things like, 'You make me so angry!' Here's a revolutionary idea: how about we instead say 'I make myself so angry in reaction to you'? That's the Buddhist perspective on emotions: it's *me* who makes myself feel these emotions.

We'll look at both of these concepts in depth later, but for now let me just mention that focusing on them changed everything for me. I accepted that my unhappiness was a reaction to the lack of control I felt over my relationship. I had no control over Adrian's emotions, but I could take responsibility for my own.

Once I stopped living in the future and faced the reality of the present moment, I knew the battle for my marriage was lost. But the battle for my *happiness* was just waiting to begin. I was the only soldier who could fight that battle, and the enemy was my readiness to blame others for my emotions.

According to Buddha, happiness is the end of suffering.

Sounds good right? Also sounds like a pretty big undertaking – to *end suffering* – particularly when you're going through the debilitating pain of a break-up (when just washing your hair feels like a major achievement!).

Let's start with just *alleviating* our suffering, shall we? Think about this in terms of taking baby steps towards feeling a little better tomorrow than you do today. We're not seeking perfection here. We're not trying to attain enlightenment in our lunch hour. We're trying to pick up the pieces after a break-up, get our lives back, and come out the other end stronger and wiser so that it'll never be this bad again. So that we might even be able to love again, albeit differently. We're trying to leave this pain behind and get onto the path of true happiness.

Buddhism is not about the end game, or perfection. It's all about the journey. Just by putting myself in Buddhism's way – as I've been doing since the mid 90s – I've learnt to walk through life with a different disposition. During that time I've oscillated between having a very intensive daily practice of Buddhist prayers and rituals to only doing light Buddhist reading, depending on how stressed I am and whether I'm ready to accept responsibility for it. When I'm really connected, I find myself walking the Earth with more confidence and peace, and I have a feeling of optimism and light-heartedness when confronted by challenges.

Separating from Adrian is the biggest challenge I've faced in my life so far, and the only thing I'm truly confident about is that focusing on Buddha's teachings, will leave me in a better place than the one in which it found me.

It's true what they say about time: it heals, if you let it. Time started working wonders for me as soon as I left the past behind and stopped recycling it every day as my present. After years of pain, I finally walked out the other side, simply by embracing and working with the present, the one time zone I can actually effect! Living in the past is the evil twin of future thinking. It blocks our view of the here and now and wastes lots of emotional energy on things we can't control. Those emotions wreak havoc on relationships in the present if we let them. My romantic relationship with Adrian is over, but I need to prevent that from negatively affecting the relationships I have with our children. Those relationships are here and now and full of love and trust. They are mine to nurture.

My overwhelming emotion now is excitement. I am excited about my future, but also excited about today – a day in which I'm out of that relationship. Today I'm not fighting for my marriage. Today I'm not trying to make someone love me, or figure out why they don't. I have a small group of close friends and family, and that is enough. Today I can have dinner with Adrian without tearing up about the future I'd planned evaporating before my eyes – and we can even have a laugh. Today I'm free, and so is he, and that is bloody brilliant.

If you've picked up this book, I'm guessing you might relate a little to the fear I felt during my marriage break-up. Maybe you're wondering whether you should break up with someone. Maybe you're already in the process of breaking up and you're in turmoil. Maybe you've broken up but you're still feeling lost. No matter where you are in the process, I know you can make it through the fear too. I only hope I can save you a little time.

I've set this book out deliberately so as to introduce you to Buddhist concepts one at a time, in the order that will likely be most helpful to you in unpacking your emotions during this confusing and intense time.

Each chapter ends with a summary of key points. I like to photocopy these sorts of things and stick them to my mirror, so that when I'm getting ready in the morning I can spend a few moments thinking about them and setting my intention for the day.

I sometimes set inspirational quotes or pointers as the wallpaper on my phone too, so that every time I check it (which is ridiculously often) I see a bit of Buddhist encouragement.

This was my favourite for a long time:

Conquer anger with non-anger.
Conquer badness with goodness.
Conquer meanness with generosity.
Conquer dishonesty with truth.

BUDDHA

So let's do this, you and I, here and now. Let's show ourselves the kindness we show our families, our friends, our pets and even our prized possessions – but rarely ourselves. Let's become the kind of person we admire – and turn a break-up into a breakthrough.

1

Buddhism 101

Before we get into the specifics of how Buddhist concepts can help you navigate a break-up, it will help to know a little about the origins of Buddhism – and about Buddha himself. So here's my short biography of Buddha, for those of you who need an introduction.

There once was an Indian prince named Siddhartha Gautama, who was born in what is now Nepal, in approximately 623 BC. The royal family into which he was born was called 'Shakya'. Later, the Sanskrit word *muni*, meaning 'able one', was added to his name, so that today, we often call this fellow Shakyamuni Buddha.

According to legend, his birth was painless and he was born with his eyes wide open. Not only that: he immediately stood up and took seven steps! His mother died some days later and he was doted on by his father, who raised him in luxury and tried to shield him from religion and any notion of human suffering. For years he was kept behind the high walls of the palace, until his curiosity finally overcame him: against his father's wishes, he commanded a servant to take him into the countryside to see how others lived.

Siddhartha didn't have to travel far to encounter the harsh reality of life outside the palace. He witnessed sickness, old age and death and realised they were coming for us all regardless of our social station or our ignorance of their existence.

The prince returned to the palace, but he couldn't see it the same way he had before. He found it hard to take joy in his life there anymore.

One night while everyone slept, Siddhartha shaved his head, swapped his clothes for rags and slipped outside the walls. Thus began his journey towards enlightenment.

Siddhartha went looking for teachers. He travelled around seeking out the most famous of them all, but none of them filled him with confidence. He didn't feel like they were able to answer his questions sufficiently, so he kept moving. Along the way, other spiritual seekers joined him. He was evidently rather charismatic, and his unanswered questions must have seemed reasonable to the others, as they decided to look for enlightenment together.

The group adopted a way of life suggested by Hindu scriptures, which recommended extreme self-denial as a means of gaining spiritual purity. We know this practice today as 'asceticism' – it is also practised by Christian priests, monks and nuns who deny themselves worldly pleasures as a form of dedication to God. Hindu ascetics tended to take on physical tasks, so Siddhartha and his friends tried inflicting pain on themselves, holding their breath for ages and fasting until they looked like walking skeletons. None of this did the trick for the prince, who couldn't shake the feeling that such acts of self-denial were as distracting as self-indulgence. He reckoned there had to be a 'middle way', without extremes, through which one could attain a peaceful-enough state to focus entirely on enlightenment.

One day Siddhartha was very weak from fasting, and asked a passing child for some rice, which she duly shared with him. Satiated, he sat down under a Bodhi tree to meditate with a clear and peaceful mind. He reached a very deep level of meditation and began realising certain truths, such as the interconnectedness of everything, and the reality of existence and suffering.

He suddenly understood that we are reborn over and over again; he saw each of his previous lives clearly. He realised that our interconnectedness reached down through lifetimes, and that our conduct determined the circumstances of our rebirths: that's what is known as 'Karma'. Moreover, he discovered that there were actually six realms of existence in which we could be born, three of which were fortunate, and three of which were unfortunate.

He became aware that reality is constantly changing, and he saw that everyone from the smallest insect to the greatest king seeks pleasure and fears displeasure. He saw the delusions we suffer and the bad consequences we create for our future selves because of them.

Finally, he saw that there was a way to end all suffering: by attaining complete clarity and understanding of the true nature of things and therefore cease the endless pursuit of pleasure and fearful running from pain.

Prince Siddhartha was enlightened.

His friends had wandered off while he was meditating, but he caught up with them about five weeks after his enlightenment and delivered his first teaching to them – the

Four Noble Truths, which are still considered the bedrock of Buddhism today. His disciples loved it! With his help, they all became enlightened; they became the first Buddhist monks. They were joined by many more, and by nuns too, and the community of monks and nuns became known as the Sangha (pronounced 'Sun-gah').

Unlike poor Jesus, Buddha was welcomed and celebrated by the kings of the day, many of whom, including his own father, became his followers. There was never any violence or persecution perpetrated against him or his students, and his community grew exponentially through word of mouth.

Buddha taught and practised freely, built monasteries and became increasingly popular and influential, while living simply and maintaining his dedication to the middle way. The only real hassles came from a couple of jealous cousins. He brushed it off pretty easily though: it's very difficult to fight with someone who refuses to let it upset them.

At the ripe old age of eighty, Buddha informed his closest followers that his life was close to completion, and soon after he became very sick with food poisoning (would you believe?). As his attendants watched, he went into the river to bathe, and then made a bed for himself on the riverbank out of leaves. He lay down on that bed, on his right side, with his right arm and hand supporting his head and his left arm lying along his left side.

Growing weaker, he gave his last teaching, urging his followers not to feel like they'd lost their master, because his teaching, the Dharma, was their master. He reminded them of their impermanence, asked them to work hard towards their enlightenment, then lost consciousness and died.

To this day you can see many reclining Buddha statues around the world: and now you know why. Next time you see one, note the serene facial expression. This is in memory of Buddha's transition into Nirvana.

Whether or not you can believe in every element of the legend of Shakyamuni Buddha and his enlightenment, the common-sense relatability of his teachings is undeniable. Here we are, two and a half thousand years later, still grappling with disturbing emotions, still wondering why bad things happen to good people and still fighting the true nature of existence.

The teachings of the Dharma bear a striking resemblance to the teachings of Jesus (who also comes with an origin story some find hard to believe), so it's hardly surprising that in the Western world – where Buddhism has been the fastest growing religion since the '50s – there is increasing overlap betwen Buddhist and Christian beliefs.

Just as the various Eastern forms of Buddhism have their own distinct flavours – from the austere and internalised Zen Buddhism of Japan to the flamboyant Tibetan Buddhism (with it's roots in Shamanism) – so too Western Buddhism is developing a personality of its own. There's no doubt that His Holiness the 14th Dalai Lama has done much to introduce the Dharma to the four corners of the globe, but the hippy generation helped too.

My friend Yeshe Khadro (or YK, as she is widely known in nickname-loving Australia) is a Buddhist nun who, among other achievements, founded the Chenrezig Institute Dharma Centre and Retreat on Queensland's Sunshine Coast and Karuna Hospice in Brisbane. She left Australia as a backpacker in 1972. Her name was Marie in those days, and although she knew little about Buddhism at that stage, she and her boyfriend signed up for a month-long Buddhist retreat as part of their overseas adventure.

Two years later she returned to Australia as an ordained Buddhist nun and she spent the next few years assuring people she hadn't joined a dangerous cult. YK is a distinctively Western Buddhist nun. She drives a car, has a job and owns a house. In other countries these are the sorts of things the Sangha sacrifice as part of their practice, but they're fed and supported by the community. If you've holidayed in a Buddhist country like Thailand or Cambodia, you might have seen monks and nuns walking the streets in the morning, holding a small bowl in front of them. Traditionally, people come out and share their food, placing it in the bowls. Today, however, people will often place money in the bowls. In fact, when I showed up at a monastery in Phnom Penh offering bread, the young monks on their mobile phones looked at me like I was some kind of country bumpkin! Our society doesn't have the same custom of supporting monks and nuns, so common sense tells us that our Sangha must live differently. YK and her peers are at the forefront of developing our own culturally relevant and sustainable kind of Buddhism.

Western Sangha are of great benefit to Western practitioners, of course, because there are sometimes cultural roadblocks between us and the high Lamas of Tibet. I'm reminded of a story I read once about a conference held near His Holiness's home in Dharamsala, India, in 1990. During a Q&A session, His Holiness was asked for direction on dealing with self-hatred.

His Holiness and his interpreter engaged in a lengthy exchange, until His Holiness said, in English and very carefully, as though he were saying the phrase for the very first time, 'Self-hatred? What is that?'

A discussion ensued in which people attempted to explain the concept to His Holiness, but he remained baffled.

'I thought I had very good acquaintance with the mind,' he said, 'but now I feel quite ignorant.'

For the life of him, the Dalai Lama couldn't understand the concept of self-hatred, because to a Tibetan Buddhist it is nonsensical. Unfortunately, it's all too real a concept in the West. This is a good example of why, as wonderful as it is to spend time with Tibetans, sometimes we need to run things by the Western robes.

For his part, His Holiness has said repeatedly, 'I do not want to convert people to Buddhism – all major religions, when understood properly, have the same potential for good.'

Many people in the West perceive Buddhism as a philosophy, rather than a religion, and continue to practise other religions while meditating on the Dharma.

Buddha is considered a teacher, not a god.

There is a commonly held misconception that His Holiness the Dalai Lama is the reincarnation of Shakyamuni Buddha. He isn't, he's the fourteen reincarnation of Chenrezig, the Buddha of Compassion. Different dude.

There are actually many Buddhas, but Shakyamuni Buddha is the most recent to appear in our world.

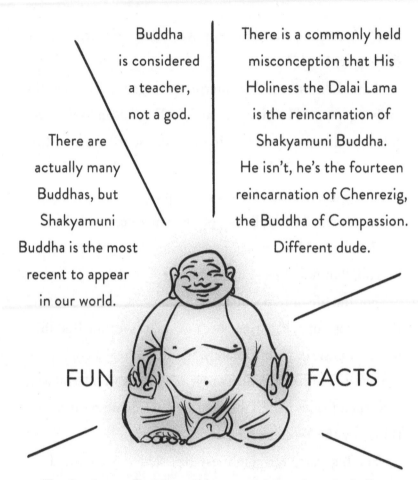

FUN FACTS

The fat, happy Buddha we see around the place, including above, isn't Shakyamuni Buddha. It's a guy called Budai, who was an eccentric monk who lived in China around 900 AD and was much loved. His image is sometimes presented as the likeness of Maitraya, a Buddha who some believe will come to earth at some stage in the future with further teachings.

2

Emptiness

When we think of breaking up, we often think of emptiness. Empty house, empty bed, empty bank account: break-ups can leave our lives feeling hollow in many ways. I genuinely believed Adrian and I would be together forever, so when it became clear to me that our relationship was over, I felt like half a person. I couldn't see what future there was for me if there wasn't a future with him. At my lowest, I wondered what point there was in getting out of bed in the morning. I felt like Adrian and our partnership had been the point of everything I'd ever done. Without him, I couldn't think of a reason to do anything at all. I felt like my life was empty of all meaning. Blimey, break-ups are dramatic, aren't they?

Obviously there's a lot of dysfunction and desperation in that kind of thinking, and a lot of fear and habit too. The thing is: this was my very first broken heart. Yes, you read that correctly. I'd never had a broken heart until I was in my forties. So I gave myself licence to go full *Eat, Pray, Love* on it. Well, Eat and Pray, at least.

Funnily enough, though, those feelings I labelled 'emptiness' at the time were actually the result of my lack of understanding of the Buddhist sense of Emptiness.

Buddha asked us to re-examine reality, to check how much of what we think of as 'real' really exists. He realised that we humans have a habit of projecting qualities onto things and people and then never checking in again to see if they've changed – or if changes in us mean we react differently to them now. Have you ever tried a food you used to think was gross – like caviar or blue cheese – and found that you now enjoy it? That's a great example of re-examining reality and finding it has changed. After a certain age, we find that even the reality of our bodies changes almost daily. I remember Judith Lucy saying on stage one night that since she turned thirty-five, tweezers had suddenly become the most important piece of equipment in her life. I totally get the tweezers thing now, but I've also recently developed 'age spots' on the back of my hands and an allergy to almonds. I mean, WTF?

We are changing all the time – which is why Buddha said there is no 'I'. There is no definitive 'me', because I'm changing every second – as is everyone and everything else. This is why we need to keep checking in with ourselves, and with everything and everyone around us. When we do that, we often find we're relating to a situation as it *used* to be, not as it is now. That's how we can feel like we're suddenly speaking a different language to everyone else.

It's hardly surprising that we humans fall back on assuming things are how they used to be. The world is a complex and confusing place that bombards us with information all the time. As a way of coping with that, we decide

Emptiness is one of the most complex concepts in Buddhism, so don't stress if it feels like it's sailing over your head at first. My advice is to do what I did through the first three seasons of *Game of Thrones*: don't overthink it, and trust that it'll all come together for you a bit later down the track. It did for me and I'm sure it will for you too.

we already know most of what's going on around us, and we stop paying attention to it.

I'm sure you've probably come across memes like this in your social media feeds.

Can you find the
the MISTAKE?
1 2 3 4 5 6 7 8 9

Of course, the mistake is that the word 'the' appears twice in the sentence. The puzzle plays on the fact that we tend to glance at things quickly, decide what they are in less than a second based on what we've known in the past, and move on to the next piece of information that needs to be sorted and filed by our brain. We tend to rely upon impressions of reality, rather than slowing down to examine things closely every single time we encounter them. This habit saves us a lot of time and effort, but it also means we miss nuanced information about the world and people around us.

I was once taken through a guided meditation that aimed to demonstrate why this is important to our survival. As we sat comfortably trying not to think about anything in particular, the instructor asked us to listen only to our breathing. Then, after a few minutes, he asked us to listen to the sounds of the room and nothing else. After that we were instructed to listen to the sounds from outside of the room and nothing else, and then to the noises from further away, like the freeway a few blocks over. After the meditation, we talked about the experience, and he asked us to imagine being aware of all of those noises, all the time. Sounds like hell, doesn't it?

Imagine being aware of what the fabric of your clothes feels like on your skin, all the time. Imagine being aware of blinking, all the time. Imagine feeling every hair on your body as they gently stand up, lie down and brush against your skin, *all the time*! I don't know about you, but that totally freaks me out, and I, for one, am very grateful to my human brain for protecting me from that information overload.

My brain allows me to focus on what I want to, which is great, but sometimes this means I miss details that would make me see the world more realistically. And the more realistically I can see the world, the more effectively I can move around in it. I often think, when I feel like I'm running into brick wall after brick wall, that I must be missing something. I mustn't be seeing the world as it really is. I felt that way in my marriage for a very long time, but I've also felt that way in other relationships. Maybe you have too?

For about the last five years of my marriage, it felt like some sort of unpredictable moving object – like a mechanical bull that I was desperately trying to stay on top of. I perceived myself as a person who hadn't changed, and saw my husband's changes as a betrayal. If I hadn't changed, and we weren't getting along anymore, then it must be all his fault, right?

When I finally started looking at the situation closely – and noticing what it really looked like – I realised that our lives were very different from the ones we'd led just a couple of years earlier. I was demanding we relate to each other as we had in the past, but we were no longer those people. That was very frustrating for Adrian, of course, and led to arguments and to both of us employing different coping mechanisms to deal with the drama: drinking for him and workaholism for me. Those coping methods created even more problems, and up she went like a bonfire on a littered Balinese beach!

After years of painful discord, I knew that if I wanted any kind of balance back in my life, I had to throw my leg over and jump down from that mechanical bull.

It took me a very long time to face the situation and really look at it and at all the factors that play a part in it.

Sometimes I think I'll spend the rest of my life trying to figure it all out, but at least I know that I'm finally really looking at things as they are – not as I assumed they were.

Everything is changing, all the time. Every single element known (and unknown) to humankind is constantly changing. From every human cell to every mountain. We learn that in primary school, but for some reason we tend not to apply it to our lives. I suppose it's probably fear-based, as most problematic behaviours are!

We accuse each other of changing like it's a terrible thing. In fact, it's inevitable, and is intrinsically neither terrible nor wonderful, but probably a bit of both.

For many years I was still trying to interact with my old impression of Adrian, rather than with the real Adrian who was standing in front of me. Even as I accepted he'd changed, my reaction was to try everything to make him change back, and that caused a great deal of suffering for both of us.

This stuff happens in friendships too, but instead of nagging and fighting about it, we tend to bitch about our besties behind their backs. You know the difference between a little bit of gossiping and full-blown bitching about someone every time their back is turned. If you're indulging in the latter – like, a lot – maybe it's time to consider whether the two of you are really still friends at all. Maybe, if you strip it back and look at the reality of the relationship you'll see you're two people who actually don't like each other or bring out the best in each other anymore. Someone who was an awesome partner in crime at twenty-six might not necessarily be your strongest emotional support at thirty-six. Not because either of you is a bad person, but because neither of you is the same person you once were. That's not only ok, it's inevitable. At some point you may need to jump off that bucking bronco of a friendship and, whether or not the other person accepts it, you can do that with love and best wishes to that person.

Buddha realised that it's unrealistic to hope for security, reliability and same-ness, let alone assume we're entitled to them. These ideas are contrary to the reality of life, which is insecure, unreliable and constantly changing. Again, we know this. Whenever we hear of a sudden death, we tell ourselves, 'It just goes to show that nothing is certain.' And yet we go on pretending life is fixed.

If we approach each person as 'empty', as though we have absolutely no information about them at all (and we don't, because they've changed since last time we saw them), we can interact with them completely in the moment, as they really are.

But it's very difficult to do that with someone we believe we know very well, especially someone we believe owes us something or has hurt us. We don't want to let them off the hook, but the truth is: we're the ones on the hook. We who hold on to the past and demand recompense, we who come back time and again, expecting the other person to make us feel better – we're the ones dangling out there, and we're the only ones who can rescue ourselves.

If we can approach a former lover, friend or family member with the idea of emptiness in our minds – that is, approach them as though we don't know who they are or what they're thinking – we can really listen and learn. Even a small new nugget of information in a difficult relationship can blow the whole thing wide open (in a good way) and create a light at the end of the tunnel of our own suffering. In my case, I had convinced myself that Adrian hated me, and that caused me unbearable pain. That assumption closed my eyes and ears to everything.

When I was eventually able to hear what Adrian was actually saying and notice the way he was actually behaving,

I realised he didn't hate me at all. Once we separated and gave each other a break from fighting, we were able to behave more like our reasonable selves again. I realised to my great relief that we could remain friends and raise our children in a friendly environment. It certainly wasn't my preference (which was for us to stay together and for Adrian to find a way to be happy with me), but it wasn't the worse case scenario either. It was a pretty positive development.

BIAS

There's another big problem with labelling things and people, and that is that we are all biased. After early childhood, when we examine everything closely, we stop looking closely at anything at all. Instead, we just apply the information we have about something similar. We activate a bias – just like we did earlier with the error in the sentence. We assumed we knew what the sentence said without actually looking at each word in it.

This human tendency would probably be less problematic if we all had the same biases, but we don't. No two people see anything in exactly the same way. What we 'see' is influenced by past experiences and what we've been taught.

The clearest example of this I can think of is the great Vegemite debate. Australians love this thick, black, salty spread made from animal byproducts. It's among the very first foods we feed our babies, and the most reliable comfort food for hungover adults. Asian resorts frequented by Australians must offer Vegemite with the breakfast buffet or face mutiny. The first thing we do when visited by someone from another country is feed them Vegemite. We do it for a laugh because we know they'll gag, scream, run for water and spend the rest of their lives talking about how disgusting it is. We are biased towards Vegemite. We've been conditioned to think it's brilliant – and we do, without reservation.

Similarly, all of us have been conditioned to value or reject certain things in other people. Within relationships, these biases can create tension around what is and isn't reasonable behaviour. While one partner may have been raised to believe that every penny is precious, the other may have come from the 'you can't take it with you' school of thought. Our biases can chip away relationships in many ways. Anyone who's had a partner who's previously been cheated on will know how that situation biases a person's attitude towards trust in a relationship. Rather than looking at you and your relationship completely afresh, your partner might instead rely upon their biased impressions of relationships and human behaviour. From their perspective, going though your phone while you're in the shower might seem like a reasonable safeguard. They might even say things like, 'Well, why do you care if you've got nothing to hide?' They might label your taking offence at their actions 'unreasonable'.

Parenting seems to release a swathe of biases that have hitherto lain dormant for many couples. Some women find themselves suddenly assuming their partners are incapable of the most basic activities. 'Useless' is a word I hear bandied about quite a bit at the school gate. Some men find themselves struggling to see their partners sexually after they become 'mums'. Our childhood observations of our parents create a biased perspective of who parents are – who *we* are as parents. In my case, my parents were both pretty vocal about what made other people 'bad' parents. This bias came back to me as sharply as the pain of a burst appendix recently, when my children told me I'd sent them to school without lunch. Their teacher had organised a lunch order for them, so they hadn't starved, but I was completely mortified, of course. In my mind's eye I could see the looks my parents used to give when they heard about such things happening back in their day.

Of course, the reality is that I am a very tired single mum with several jobs, and accidents happen. That's all it is, but my bias helped me label it a complete disaster and a disgrace! I came down very hard on myself all afternoon for being a dead-beat mum and had a quiet cry in the shower about it that night, thus creating hours of suffering for myself from something that had been resolved by 9.15 that morning. Dumb.

We apply our bias, and then decide on a definition of everything and everyone around us. We commit ourselves 100 per cent to that definition. We believe it is real and we call it the truth. That, according to Buddha, is our delusion. As we humans wander around, bumping into each other with our conflicting truths, we often can't even agree on the way things are, let alone what to do about them, and that causes us suffering.

This is how those frustrating one-sided arguments arise in which one partner is completely incensed and the other has literally no idea why! It's very difficult to find any resolution to an argument only one person understands. Frustration builds on both sides, people accuse each other of being crazy, and before you know it you're creating lots of other dramas to fight about. Suffering, suffering, suffering!

Buddha suggested we try dropping our delusions. He said we should aspire to Emptiness — to approaching everything and everyone with no prior preconceptions. He said we should approach them that way every single time.

Famous scholar and yogi Khenpo Tsultrim Gyamtso Rinpoche puts it this way:

See the true nature, then let go and relax into that.

This sentiment really rings true to me. I was so anxious for so long about what my life would look like if I accepted the true nature of my relationship with Adrian. But once I took the leap and really looked at it, most of the anxiety dropped away. Things are rarely as bad as we fear they'll be. The more calm and relaxed we are, the more skilfully we can interact with the world around us. Once I relaxed into the true nature of my current relationship with Adrian, I was able to see there was still a lot to value in it, and we could start working on our friendship.

THE GREATEST DELUSION
(Buddha's 'bout to blow your mind, yo!)

Let's get back to this idea of the self, the 'I'. According to

Buddha, the greatest delusion of all is the self, the idea that I am a completely independent being.

> Enlightenment for a wave in the ocean is the moment the wave realises that it is water.
>
> THICH NHAT HANH

What Buddha wants us to do, ideally, is to have the same feelings for every single living being on the planet, including ourselves. Jesus was into this too, and he put it this way: 'Love your neighbour as you love yourself.'

Both Buddha and Jesus observed that we humans tend to put ourselves in the middle of our universe and then categorise others into gradually larger orbits of importance around us. So in terms of who I love and wish to protect, it goes: me, then my immediate family, then my extended family, then my neighbours, my class, my countrymen, my race and so on.

Both teachers thought it unwise for us to see ourselves as being part of exclusive groups like that. They thought that was a fundamental misunderstanding of reality that leads to selfishness and greed. When we put borders up around ourselves, we naturally start to think of those outside those borders as less important than those inside. At worst, we can see the outsiders as threatening. We see their happiness and safety as less important than those of the people inside our borders. I might punch my neighbour in the nose for parking in my driveway, but protest beside him to prevent refugees from moving into our community. (I wouldn't do either of those things, but you get the picture.) My loyalty depends on which ring of orbit is being threatened. Sometimes I wish for an alien invasion, so that the human species could be galvanised against a common enemy, but if *Game of Thrones* has taught me anything, it's that we humans will keep fighting our little ego battles no matter what existential crisis looms on our horizon.

We're even prepared to risk the lives of outsiders just to keep conditions inside the borders predictable. Life inside the borders may not be perfect, but at least it's reliable we tell ourselves. Why risk changing it by allowing others in? Even if they might die out there, we have to protect ourselves, right? Well the problem with that is that the outsiders *are* ourselves. They are us. We might be waves, but we are also water.

Here's where it all comes together and we start talking about break-ups again. Pairing up with someone in a relationship is the ultimate creation of an exclusive group, and because we're human, we tend to take it way too far. We see that group as an actual thing that exists, independently of everything else. Often we lose track of other friends when we couple up, we see less of our parents or siblings, and we spend more and more time in the company of that one special person. This is the period through which we build up the trust and connection within the couple, we share secrets, plan the fulfilment of dreams and create an 'us against the world' closeness that makes us feel safe. We build a border around ourselves.

With the border comes the pressure. We start to hold our partner responsible for our happiness, our esteem and our success. Our biases come into play, and we expect our partners to act in certain ways, ways that we think people in love should act. We fill the gaps with projections. We see what we want to see, and ignore what we don't like, or resolve to change it.

We expect our partner to give us everything we want and need and we burden them with our every wobble in confidence. We ask them to fix us when we're broken. If they don't know what to do, we accuse them of not loving us enough, or of 'changing'. As we grow older together, we find some of our dreams haven't come true, and we blame each other for not trying hard enough or being supportive enough. We might chafe under the weight of them and create secret outlets for ourselves.

We expect more from our partner than from any other person on Earth, and when they fail to live up to our expectations, we curse them.

After a while of feeling unhappy, I shifted my view of Adrian from 'he is the best person in the world', straight to 'he is the worst person in the world'. I wanted to hurry up and get happy, so I kicked him out. This was about three years before our eventual permanent split, and it played out very differently.

I wasn't really ready to break up. Rather, I was trying to scare Adrian, to manipulate him into being the person I wanted him to be. I felt he was wilfully being an arsehole by being unhappily married to me, and could just as easily be perfect (and perfectly happy) if only he'd choose to be. I thought that with the right motivation – seeing that he could potentially lose his family and the lifestyle we'd built together – he'd come to his senses.

I still wanted some control over him though – I didn't want him to wander too far away – so I rented him a flat nearby. I put the utilities in my name and set up direct debits to pay them. I gave him twelve months to sort himself out, by which I meant start being nice to me again (he didn't think he had anything to sort out), after which he would either move back in with us or go on his way without my assistance. I never believed for a moment he would get his act together to make a life for himself without me, and I let him know that.

This was a very manipulative plan of action. In Buddhist terms, it was graspy, craving, attached behaviour, which we'll talk about in the next chapter. I was clinging to our old relationship, which didn't actually exist anymore. As you can see, I was very far from approaching the situation with an open – empty – mind.

In her essay 'Dependent Arising and Emptiness', Australian nun Robina Courtin said:

> One way of describing what Buddha's talking about is that everything in our mind is a viewpoint, is an opinion, is an attitude, is an interpretation. Everything in our mind is a viewpoint, is an interpretation of the people and things and events and self that are the occupants of our lives. Everything is view. Everything is how we see things.

I had very strong views, opinions and biases about our relationship, and they were very different to Adrian's views, opinions and biases. Perhaps we'd have had a better chance if I'd been able to understand and articulate it so clearly at the time. What I actually did was send nasty texts and threaten a lot.

My views were preventing me from seeing our relationship as it actually was. I was clinging to an image of who I thought Adrian was which prevented me from really seeing him. It was all caught up with some deeply imbedded delusions about our past relationship, and our past selves. In my memory, our past relationship had been perfect and I wanted what I remembered back. Nothing else would do.

As you can probably tell, at this time I was kind of hysterical. I forgot to focus on the Dharma. When I did remember it, I knew it would tell me I was doing everything wrong, and I just wasn't ready to face up to that at the time.

If only I'd gone back to Buddha's definition of Emptiness, I'd have seen that Adrian wasn't hurting me by changing, and he wasn't changing himself just to hurt me. I was hurting myself by trying to hold on to something that no longer existed.

At the end of the twelve months, Adrian and I got back together. We'd had intensive couples counselling, but I was still deluded and unready to let go of my biased views. I should say that our wonderful counsellor, James, told me straight that he thought I was deluded about the future of the relationship, as did my mother, my mower man and several psychics. I was determined to push on, though, in no small part because my parents are still together, and I have some heavy biases about 'giving up' on a marriage.

Going through the counselling encouraged me to return to Buddhism, which overlaps with modern psychology on many levels. As our counsellor worked with us on things like ego and expectation, I dusted off some of my old books and got working on myself again. This work didn't 'save' our marriage, but it certainly laid the groundwork for us to eventually carry out a very different break-up from the first.

Focusing on Emptiness allowed me to look at Adrian as he actually was now, with increasing clarity, and without thinking he should still be who he was in the past. For a while, I often got a bit of a shock when I interacted with him, as though I was looking in the mirror and seeing an unfamiliar face reflected back at me. That's how well I thought I knew him – as well as I knew my own face. I also thought I knew his mind as well as I knew my own, but for a couple of years I'd been finding myself increasingly out of step with him, and him increasingly unpredictable. I had blamed him for that shock and reacted angrily.

'Why are you being like this?' I'd yell.

'Like what?' he'd reply angrily.

What I meant was: 'Why aren't you doing what I thought you'd do?'

What he meant was: 'Because this is who I am right now.'

Focusing on Buddha's teaching about Emptiness meant approaching Adrian without an expectation of who he was (or who I *thought* he was) and accepting whoever he turned out to be. That, in turn, meant accepting that I might not love the person I encounter.

Let's go back over that, because it's been the key to my recovery from heartache, and I want to make sure you get it, in case it's yours too.

I worked very hard at seeing Adrian as he actually is, and not as I expected him to be. Have you ever seen a photo or video of yourself that freaked you out because you appeared a lot older, greyer, fatter or balder than you imagine yourself to be? We all walk around with an image in our minds of what we look like, but sometimes we're faced with the reality that our self-image is outdated. That person doesn't exist anymore. The funny thing is that we can look at our partner every day of our lives and not notice the changes taking place in them either.

My dad still talks about my mum's 'lovely pins', meaning her legs. Mum reckons in his mind's eye he still sees her legs as they were forty-five years ago. That's an example of how delusion can work in a relationship's favour!

In my case, though, I had to accept that Adrian was not only a different man to the one I still saw when I looked at him, but a man I was no longer compatible with. I kept asking myself, 'Would I fall in love with Adrian if I met him today?' The answer, for many reasons, was 'no'. I kept saying to him, accusingly, 'You're not the man I married,' as though it was his responsibility to regress twenty years. The fact is, if we were to meet for the first time now, I doubt we'd be able to sustain much of a conversation, let alone think about dating each other.

I used to get so angry about our incompatibility. How could it just happen? How could I reverse it? How could Adrian reverse it? Why was he choosing to be this person I didn't love? I was very angry about the fact that I didn't love the person I was encountering, but when I emptied out my expectations, I realised there was no reason to be angry. I'm not angry when I meet a perfect stranger for the first time and don't love them, so if I really embrace and accept Emptiness I won't feel anger when I don't find Adrian lovable either.

This is the second part of my personal recovery – respecting and accepting who Adrian is now, even though I'm not in love with him.

I have to respect Adrian, because our children depend on me doing so. Would I bother pushing myself to that level of personal development if it weren't for them? Probably not. I'd probably deal with the pain of breaking up by trying to never see him again, but that's not an option for me, and frankly it would be my loss if it were. The longer we live apart, the more able I am to like Adrian again. In fact, I have to be very careful not to fall into the trap of thinking I love him again. There are times still, when I look at him and see my old delusion. I want so badly to see it and go with it, but luckily I have my own home to go to, with my own Buddhist strategies to get me back into the here and now.

Instead of eating my heart out and allowing my mind to drift over memories, I try to discipline myself to see Adrian and the situation as they really are, and it helps a lot. Increasingly, I'm able to say to myself, 'This is okay. I don't actually want to share a bed, a bank account, a car and a life with this person. He's not a bad person, but I don't want to deal with him every day of my life. I don't agree with him on a number of important issues and I don't want to have to compromise with him. I want my independence!'

Adrian simply *isn't* the person I met and fell in love with twenty years ago. Neither am I. Neither are any of us – because we are still arising.

Buddha realised that everything in the world – every creature, every element – is constantly changing. This concept is called Impermanence, and we need only try to think of something that doesn't change to realise it's true. Even the hardest rock is being constantly carved away by the wind and rain. Similarly, we humans are being constantly carved away by our experiences in life. We can try to control that process to a certain extent, by developing emotional discipline, which is what Buddha advocated, but even then we have to accept there'll be things beyond our control that will change us. They'll change our environment and the people we love. Our constant changing, our evolution or *arising*, is dependent on the elements and events around us. Each element and event is dependent on the elements and events around it. So we can see that everything is connected. Everything is influencing everything else.

We are all *dependently arising*. We are all evolving constantly in response to everyone and everything else, and we are affecting everyone and everything else as they evolve too. Phew!

I've definitely thrown you in at the philosophical deep end here, but don't be put off. If Buddhism was a step aerobics class, Dependent Arising, Impermanence and Emptiness would be a diagonal K-step with repeater and a reverse turn into a helicopter. You won't have to perform it very often and there'll be a hell of a lot of basics and grapevines in between. Don't worry!

IMPERMANENCE

the understanding that everyone and everything in the world is constantly changing

I bring this up now because Dependent Arising, Impermanence and Emptiness are core concepts of Buddha's philosophy. Everything else relates back to them (you'll quickly notice that when it comes to Buddhism everything relates to everything else!).

DEPENDENT ARISING

the understanding that we never stop evolving and changing, and that our evolution is shaped by the conditions around us

It's often said that Emptiness and Impermanence are two sides of the one coin. We need to accept that everything is constantly changing, still arising, not set forever in the same shape and form. Accepting that enables us to look on things with fresh eyes, and with Emptiness. When we look with Emptiness, we're not shocked or angered when things and people are different from how they were before, because we don't expect them to stay the same. We can make smarter decisions, because we see things clearly. We're not distracted by the shock of the new.

We ask children to try things over and over because we know how much our feelings and attitudes have changed since childhood, but for some reason we believe our adult attitudes are inherently correct and set in stone. When we change our minds about something, we are reluctant to admit it because it seems wishy-washy – it's as if we are admitting we were, God forbid, *wrong* about something. Once we realise the reality of Impermanence, changing our minds is so much easier, because we know that everything is constantly changing. In fact, the idea of not changing our minds seems a bit silly and stubborn.

Eventually, as I read various books and listened to YouTube teachings and podcasts about Emptiness and

Impermanence and reflected on them, I felt truly ready to look at my life afresh. I held my nose, squeezed my eyes shut and dive-bombed into the truth of my marriage, while trying with everything I had not to imagine what it would look, sound, taste or smell like. I had to try to experience it as it really was, with Emptiness and without expectation.

What I found were two nice people who were both trying really hard, and yet were still driving each other crazy. I couldn't help thinking both of them deserved some peace in their lives. When we recalibrate our outlook by incorporating Buddha's teaching about Emptiness and Impermanence, we can drop the problematic labels we put on people and things.

I was no longer burdened by the ways in which I'd been describing Adrian and our marriage to myself. Where once my inner monologue had been filled with sad, hateful and resentful words that kept me in a dark and miserable place, I was suddenly able to fill my mind with positive, practical and encouraging words and thoughts. I was able to think about positive aspects of breaking up with Adrian, and for the first time in ages I was able to rally some actual excitement about my future.

When you first start exploring Emptiness, you have to be careful. The great Buddhist teacher Nagarjuna said, 'Emptiness wrongly grasped is like picking up a poisonous snake by the wrong end.' I remember my first tentative steps into Buddhist literature, which took place in the internet-free dark ages of the early 1990s (at least they were internet-free for *me*). The first two concepts I came across were Attachment and Emptiness. After some very rudimentary skimming on both subjects, I came away thinking Buddhism was about not loving anyone and believing nothing mattered. I'd definitely grabbed the wrong end of the snake! Luckily, I persevered. In Buddhist terms, Emptiness isn't the nihilistic dead-end it may seem to be at first. On the contrary: it can really give you a new lease on life.

We must push ourselves to revisit our attitudes about our relationships. Assuming you love someone because you loved them a long time ago may be a problem. On the other hand, deciding there is no good whatsoever to an ex-partner may also be causing you trouble. Perhaps your attitude about being single or divorced has been carved into a very tight, unyielding negative shape that's making your break-up hard to move past.

KEY POINTS

- Emptiness is profound open-mindedness. It is approaching things and people without expectation, seeing them as they really are now, in this moment, not as you expect or remember them to be.

- Dependent Arising is the backbone of Buddhism. It is the understanding that we never stop evolving and changing, and that our evolution is shaped by the conditions around us. Those conditions are always changing too, and are shaped by the conditions around them. Everything is connected and influencing everything else. Nothing and no-one is the same as the last time we saw them, and definitely not the same as the first time we saw them.

- As you and your partner change, the honest truth is that you may not love the person your partner actually is now. They will continue to change, but they will never change *back*, and neither will you.

- Labels are meaningless and get in the way of seeing people and things clearly.

- Explore your real feelings today. Don't just assume they are as they were before. Work on emptying out your old ideas and approach situations with Emptiness.

SELF-REFLECTION

As we progress though *Buddhism for Break-ups*, I'll ask you to try to 'empty out' your old ideas about a lot of things. I'll walk you through a new way of thinking about yourself and the world around you, in the hope that you'll be able to move out of this break-up phase of your life and on towards happiness and peace.

Take some time to think about the following questions. Make some notes about how they make you feel and what your answers might be. We'll revisit these notes towards the end of the book and see if anything has changed for you.

If you're thinking about breaking up with someone, ask yourself these questions:

- What part are you playing in the problems in the relationships?

- How does your partner make you feel?
  (Trick question alert!)

- What's the biggest thing you're scared of losing?

- What advantages might there be to the break-up?

- Are you depressed and/or anxious? About what exactly?

If you've gone through a break-up with someone, ask yourself these questions:

- Are you still in love with your ex, and would you want to reconcile?

- What was your part in the breakdown of the relationship?

- How does your ex make you feel? (Trick question alert!)

- What's the biggest thing you've lost in the break-up?

- Are there any advantages to the break-up?

- What does life look like now?

- Are you depressed and/or anxious? About what exactly?

3

Attachment

> The root of all suffering is attachment.
>
> BUDDHA

'Woah there, Buddha!' I hear you say. 'The root of *my* suffering is that I'm *no longer* attached!'

I hear you, but stay with me (and Buddha), because like Emptiness, Attachment is a very different beast when viewed through Buddhist eyes.

Honestly, this is probably the teaching I refer to most often, to make my life easier in lots of ways. It's a corker.

In daily life, when we say someone is 'attached' to us – or we're 'attached' to them – it's usually seen as a compliment and a positive development in a relationship. If anything, we're more likely to view *de*tachment in relationship as the sign of a problem. The feeling that Adrian was pulling away, or detaching, from me definitely started the ball rolling in our break-up.

I'll be honest with you, when I first read that Buddha believed we shouldn't be attached to anyone, I thought I'd stumbled into one of those terrifying cults where you're not allowed to love anyone or have birthday parties. Thankfully I kept reading

ATTACHMENT
(Upadana) Grasping, clinging, craving

and discovered that this is one of the many common misunderstandings arising from translation quirks when we encounter with Buddhism.

The early Buddhist scriptures were written in the Pali and Sanskrit languages, and often there are no precise English translations. These scriptures refer to *Upadana*, which most closely translates as 'attachment', 'clinging' or 'grasping'. 'Grasping' probably gives us the best idea of the kind of attachment Buddha's worried about. He never instructed us not to love people; in fact, he'd prefer it if we loved absolutely everyone! But he didn't want us to 'grasp' at them, long for them or obsess over them.

Buddha never asked us not to have relationships with other people. He never suggested we shouldn't love people, or enjoy things or activities. What he said was that craving – whether for people or things – brings us negative consequences. I suppose the amount of angst a relationship causes us is a pretty good indication of how much grasping is going on.

Buddha went so far as to say that Attachment is the root of all suffering, for two reasons. First, he thought it represented a fundamental misunderstanding of reality. As we know, thanks to dependent arising, Buddha believed that everything is interconnected. Every person, animal and plant is dependent on the conditions around it for it's birth and survival; everything is dependent on everything else. Everything is related to everything else and everything is united. So according to Buddha, we don't have to grasp for people or things: we're already connected to them. Pushing for some kind of exclusive, extra-special connectedness is where we run into trouble. This harks back to our previous discussion about building walls around ourselves.

Second, Buddha felt that being attached to or grasping for people or things ultimately leads to disturbing emotions that cause us suffering, and those emotions lead to regrettable behaviour that causes us more suffering. Let's look at how that can happen.

I had an old view of my relationship that went like this: 'Adrian dotes on me and does everything I want. He will never break up with me, no matter what.' That was a very outdated opinion of Adrian, which showed my ignorance of impermanence. It wouldn't do me any good to continue thinking of him and interacting with him from that standpoint. I needed to approach him with Emptiness, to see who he actually was now, who he'd evolved into, if I wanted to avoid a very rude shock. But for a while I refused to let that view go. I was attached to it, and that attachment brought me a lot of suffering.

I still continually have to empty out my old views of Adrian and approach him anew. We are connected, not least through our two children. If I ignore that fact, or can't see it because my emotions are clouding my perspective, I might panic and try to drag him closer to me. Who wants to be closer to a panicking, deluded, grasping mess?

It's analogy time. Imagine you and a friend are taking a rollercoaster ride together. You get strapped into seats beside each other, low and tight and completely solid, unified and safe; you're like one with the machine and with each other. Then, as the ride moves off, the other person grabs you, grasps for you, clings to you like they want to crawl inside you. They claw your skin and scream your name. This experience (otherwise known as going to Luna Park with my mum) shows they've fundamentally misunderstood the reality of the situation – you are safe and connected. Their behaviour is not helpful and it's not making anyone safer or happier. As you try to avoid their grasping, scrabbling and screaming, they panic even more and their behaviour becomes crazier and crazier – which of course leads to you pulling even harder to get away. It's a pretty uncomfortable cycle.

Attachment, in the Buddhist sense of *Upadana*, is a symptom of the fundamental misunderstanding of the unity of all things. There is no need to grasp for anything, because nothing is separate from you. Grasping doesn't draw you any closer. If anything, it tends to push people away and/or create situations in which they feel as though they have to lie to you and manipulate you, just to be with you.

We all have someone in our lives whose name elicits groans when it appears as an incoming call on our phone, right? Maybe we lie to that person about our plans because he or she is so draining to be around. Unfortunately, that sort of game-playing usually only leads to more grasping on their part – and more calls!

The people we tend to enjoy spending time with are generally relaxed in our company. They are happy to see us, but they don't stress about how long we'll stay or when they'll see us again. They don't grasp at us, but let us sit comfortably with them, enjoying the connection of that moment without fretting about the next one, or grasping for reassurance.

Craving leads to all sorts of troubles – just ask any woman on a diet! Ask anyone who's struggled with addiction. These kinds of attachments affect us in the same ways as our attachment to people. These are all forms of grasping, making us unhappy and irrational.

Because we convince ourselves that we need other people and things to be happy, we can very easily go through life feeling like we never have enough. No matter how much we have, we crave – and grasp for – more.

The next time you are agitated or upset, please do me a favour. Ask yourself, 'What am I attached to?' Or, in other words, 'What do I think should be happening right now, and isn't? What craving is going unfulfilled?'

I was having quite a good day recently – feeling ok about my break-up, on top of things, even happy. Then I bumped into a friend who told me her 18-year-old daughter was off on her first overseas trip – to Hungary, France, Italy and Germany.

'Oh, I love Germany,' I said to my friend, and then all of a sudden, without warning, a panicked craving enveloped me.

Years ago, before kids, Adrian and I visited Germany together – twice in fact. We toured around for weeks and had a brilliant time. His family history is tied up with World War II so he's always taken an interest in Germany. He never thought he'd ever set foot in any of the places his grandmother spoke so vividly about during his childhood, but I made it my mission to get us there. We were both overwhelmed by the achievement, as neither of us came from families who ever even considered overseas holidays. We couldn't believe we'd done it, and it was a very special, bonding experience. We resolved to return there one day, but next time we'd bring our as yet unborn children, rent a flat and stay for a year or two.

These plans came flooding back to me in that moment. The pain of the realisation that they would never happen was sharp. It brought tears to my eyes. What *was* my future then? What was left of the dreams I'd had? I was suddenly flailing: grasping.

In this case the thing I was attached to was obvious: I was grasping for the future I used to think I had. But it's not always so obvious what the attachment is. Generally, I have to stop myself and ask, 'Why ...?'

'Why am I kicking the washing machine?'

The first answer may be, 'Because it's leaking.'

I dig a little deeper. 'Because now I have to go through the hassle of organising a repair.'

Deeper still: 'Because I have to do everything around here since I'm alone with no-one to care for me.'

Aha! I'm kicking the washing machine because I'm craving having another adult in the house again. I'm craving having someone show they care for me by helping me. I'm attached to the idea that I shouldn't have to deal with this stuff alone, that Adrian should be here taking care of me the way I want to be taken care of, and the way I thought he always would. I'm attached to Adrian and I need to get over it. That's the real reason I'm kicking the washing machine.

For the sake of the washing machine and various other inanimate objects around my home that cop a kick every now and then, I need to deal with Attachment. Here are some other reasons why dealing with it is a good idea.

- Attachment makes it very difficult to cultivate contentment, because there's always more to have and better versions of what you've got already. In terms of a relationship, attachment to being spoiled or told we're loved can lead to craving more and more of that lovely stuff. It becomes hard for our partner to keep up with. We can end up resentful about very minor infractions! Attachment to sex can create some unrealistic benchmarks too.

- Attachment makes us moody, as we swing between the exhilaration of getting something we've been craving and the disappointment when it runs out again or when we feel sick from overindulging in it. Sometimes we don't end up getting what we want at all, which can be very difficult and make us ask 'What's wrong with me?' It can convince us that nothing goes right for us, that we're born unlucky, that we're victims of life itself. This outlook can become very tiring for a partner, especially if we expect them to keep topping us up and threaten grumpiness if they fail.

- By focusing on the things we are trying to get, we can miss the wonderful things that are actually happening.

- Attachment causes fear. We fear separation from people and things we desire, and fear makes us do crazy things, like ignore all the reasons why those people and things aren't good for us.

• Attachment gives people and things control over us.

• Attachment keeps us surrounded by conditions that have a negative effect on our arising – on the ways in which we are evolving. It's not hard to imagine how attachment to a bad relationship can turn us into a sad, bitter person. Or how letting go of it can help make us happier.

DEALING WITH ATTACHMENT

Of course it all comes back to Emptiness and Impermanence. We need to empty out our bank of preconceptions about what *should* be happening, and what we *should* have, and see things and people as they actually are, right now, in this moment. Then we can be honest about our feelings and make clear decisions.

There's a lot you can do to start that process. This is by no means an exhaustive checklist, but it's the list I use to help myself through episodes of craving-related craziness. I hope you find it a helpful starting point.

1. **Accept it's going to be hard.** Breaking up makes us feel lonely and unloved. I don't know about you, but I sometimes fear I'll feel that way for the rest of my life, so grasping is probably a pretty predictable reaction. Our instinct when we feel alone and vulnerable is to reach out and grab someone, and to hold onto them with all our might. That's a bad idea, but fighting that instinct is not easy. However, it will be worth it.

> One man can conquer a thousand times thousand men in battle, but one who conquers himself is the greatest of conquerors.
>
> BUDDHA

2. **Work on your awareness.** This process is also known as *mindfulness*, or the 'Why am I kicking the washing machine?' test. What am I attached to? What am I craving? If you keep trying, you'll get to the point where you'll be able to slip this step in before you freak out. I'm not talking years here, by the way. You'll be amazed how all this stuff will start to kick in as you read and think

about it more. Its practical, life-changing applications aren't that hard to harness. Just try to remain gently aware of things and don't be afraid or embarrassed to ask for a minute to collect your thoughts when you feel a freak-out coming on. In the case of the washing machine, or any other inanimate object you wish you could hurt, ask *yourself* for a minute. Walk away.

3. **Really spend some time and effort thinking about what it is you're craving.** In our case it probably feels like it's more a matter of 'who' we're craving, but when you think about it, there are a lot of things to crave after a break-up. The person we're missing represents a lot of plans, hopes, dreams, security and a sense of identity that we've spent a lot of mental energy on. They can take an awful lot with them when they leave, and we can be tempted to want them back, not for themselves but for the fantasies we built around them.

   Assess intellectually what it would do for you if you got back together. Do you really want that? Does that relationship even really exist? His Holiness the Dalai Lama puts it this way: 'Most of our troubles are due to our passionate desire for and attachment to things that we misapprehend as enduring entities.' He is touching on Impermanence here too. He's saying that everything and everyone is constantly changing. We spend a lot of time and energy craving things that won't exist forever. They may not even exist next year or tomorrow, so what's the point? In many cases, like mine, they have already ceased to exist.

The Adrian who I am craving doesn't actually exist. He kind of used to, when we were younger, but he left a long time ago. The Adrian that exists now drives me up the wall! I do not want to live with him, much less be married to him (sorry, mate!). No doubt our problems would have followed us to Germany if we'd stayed together and fulfilled that dream. It would never have been as idyllic as I imagined it. And the truth is, he probably wouldn't have lifted a finger to help me with the leaking washing machine if he had been here, so both of those emotional chain-reactions were based on nothing.

4. **Assess intellectually the positives of not having what you're craving** – i.e. the partner you no longer have. Is it saving you money? Is it sparing you emotional energy and tears? Do you get to watch the TV shows you like? Does

it mean never having to see an in-law again? There are always positives.

5. **Don't react the same way you always react just because it's the same way you always react.** You don't have to cry because you always cry, or give up because you always give up. And you don't have to get back together because you always do. Try to remember your new approach when someone else presents you with their same old behaviour. You don't have to play out the scene the same way it's always gone. Notice how differently it ends up when you approach it calmly, without attachment to scoring the same old points.

6. **Do some good for someone else.** Look beyond yourself and take your focus off your own cravings. It's hard to feel unlucky or to focus on your own problems when you're looking into the helpless and pleading face of a dog that's been abused and dumped, or distributing donated sanitary products to refugee women, or feeding the homeless. I dare say it'll help you focus on the aspects of your life that *are* working and on the ways in which you are very lucky.

If you are too busy to add anything to your schedule, perhaps you could spare a couple of minutes to commit acts of kindness on social media or at work. Wish someone happy birthday, comment on someone's photo, congratulate someone on their great news, tell them they look great. It doesn't take much, but it can make a big difference to your own outlook as well as theirs.

7. **Remember that your life is not infinite.** It will last for a certain period of time and then it will be over. How much of it do you want to spend wishing things, or people, were different? How much of it do you want to spend in an unhealthy relationship? What (and who) are you missing out on right now because you're still attached to your plans that will never happen? Sorry, I know that's heavy, but it's reality. How much of your life have you wasted on this relationship? Is it the first one you've wasted time on? It's never too late to stop wasting time.

8. **Acknowledge these changes in behaviour as you remember to make them.** Congratulate yourself and allow yourself to feel good about putting some effort into

your own happiness. You're actively pursuing personal and spiritual growth, and that is excellent. Well done.

Ultimately, attachment in a relationship has more to do with what you're craving than with the other person. It's about fulfilling *your* desires, even if it feels like all you get out of it is pain. For you to stay in a relationship, it must be serving you in some way. If you feel like your relationship wasn't serving you at all, then have a hard look at how long you stuck it out, and why. For example, if you realise you stayed because you were afraid of being alone, then you need to work on being alone so you never find yourself repeating that relationship again.

Love without Attachment is love that meets in the middle. It's love in which neither party is asking to be healed or completed. It's real and it's possible, and once you've learnt the difference, you'll never look back.

LOVING WITHOUT ATTACHMENT

In a relationship without Attachment, we are able to enjoy our time with someone and enjoy their attention without demanding more. Removing the Attachment from a relationship might be the difference between a bad romance and a great friendship. That's surely the aim of every separating couple with children.

There are lots of things I like – admire, even – about the Adrian who exists now. He's even-tempered, honest, generous, kind, creative, principled and he's a fantastic father, just to name a few. The aim of the game for both of us is to focus on the great things we see in each other, as we really are now, without angrily grasping for the things we don't see.

I know it's possible, because I've learnt to do it with my female friends.

For most of my life I've had a best friend. Not the same one, mind you. Like Leonardo Di Caprio working his way through a Victoria's Secret catalogue, the minute one of my intense friendships dissolved, I moved on to another one. Like Leo, I was never lonely, but unlike Leo (I suspect), I never felt great about it. I generally felt a bit trapped and bullied.

As far back as I can remember in childhood it was the same. I would put everything I had into just one other person. I suppose I enjoyed the exclusivity of having one strong friendship. It was nice to have a person to call my own. A person everyone else knew to be *my* best friend. It helped create an identity and it let others know that I was worthy of best friendship. (There are echoes here of my fast attachment to Adrian, and my pride in his loving me.)

Almost without exception, my best friendships were actually built on a fair bit of negativity and back-biting. Looking back now, I realise that with all of these girls and women I wasn't really a friend, but a frenemy. We both were, in every case. I would always wish my friend was different, that our friendship was different, and yet time and again I was attracted to the same kind of women: ball-breaking, over-bearing alpha females whom other people were a bit scared of. I suppose I thought that if I could tame them and become their number-one friend, it meant good things about me. I realise now that all it meant about me was that I was a manipulative, grasping, love-bombing frenemy.

A frenemy is someone you think of as a friend even though you don't actually like much about them. In fact, your frenemy's ultimate humiliating downfall is your greatest wish. I know it's unbelievable to some people, by which I mean straight men, but frenemyship is a very common phenomenon.

It's quite complicated emotionally though. If a frenemy confided in me, in that moment I would feel flattered and swear with all my heart that her secret was safe with me. The trouble was that when she wasn't around, I was flattered by the attention of other frenemies dying to know her secret. I used what I knew as currency to ingratiate myself with others, as they did with me, and round and round it went. I knew my secrets would be shared just as I shared other people's, and yet in my weakest moments, when I needed to unburden myself and feel cared for, I divulged them.

All of us were grasping at each other for attention, affection or social superiority and using each other's weaknesses to get it. Tina Fey's brilliant movie *Mean Girls* is all about this kind of female relationship. Although the film's set in a high school, in my case the pattern continued into my thirties.

I'd been studying Buddhism for a couple of years when I started to feel uneasy about my closest friendship. I blamed my friend for the fact that I sometimes hated her for sometimes being very rude to me. I blamed her for my feelings being hurt when she spoke rudely to me in front of others, and I took great pride in others remarking on her rudeness to me later. I deluded myself into thinking I was a better person than she was and a victim of her behaviour. I was jealous of her achievements and enjoyed her jealousy of mine. I very much enjoyed bitching about her when she wasn't around!

Her behaviour was pretty negative, there's no denying it, but my reaction wasn't exactly saintly. I started speaking rudely to her. I told other people things she'd have preferred I didn't. I tried to keep her away from some of my endeavours so that I wouldn't have to share my success with her. I encouraged other people's rejection of her.

After years of this sort of behaviour, neither of us was happy or content, neither was more popular and no-one came out on top in our battle for supremacy over the other. What we both ended up with was a bad reputation. People just thought we were a pair of toxic bitches!

We were miserable husks of women, working in jobs we hated, making personal decisions we regretted and oscillating between lying to each other about it all to save face and crying to each other because no-one else was interested in our drama. We were both very attached to each other, and to our identity as best friends, but we kind of ended up overwhelming ourselves with negativity in each other's names.

Luckily, around that time I started a new course at my local Buddhist centre. It was a class about disturbing emotions, and our teacher began by talking about people whom we react badly to. People we believe make us unhappy. He introduced the revolutionary concept that no-one can *make* us unhappy. We choose how we respond to other people's behaviour. They have no power over our emotions at all.

Buddha said, 'Sure, Fred punched you in the nose, but that's his problem. Yours is the anger.'
VENERABLE ROBINA COURTIN

Buddha said that no-one else can *make* us angry, or sad, or anything else for that matter. We choose how we react to the world around us. If we choose to become angry with Fred for punching us in the nose, then it follows that we can choose not to. Some of us will punch him back, some of us will walk away and resolve to deal with him when we've both calmed down. That's the difference we're talking about here: the hot reaction and the cool reaction.

The cool reaction comes from the work we're doing on dealing with Attachment. Remember, when we master the art of giving ourselves a minute to collect our thoughts, catching our negative emotions before they erupt into regrettable decisions and behaviour, we can figure out where they're really coming from and what we're actually grasping for. Then we can choose how to respond using logic and achieve a better outcome for ourselves.

As I sat in class, pondering the revolutionary thought that I was making myself unhappy, a classmate raised her hand. She described in great detail a difficult friendship that had been part of her life for longer than I'd been alive. Without batting an eyelid, our teacher asked, 'Can you end it?'

The pupil was stunned by the question. 'Can I end the friendship?' she asked.

'Sure,' replied our teacher. 'Why not? You don't seem to like this lady. You could work very hard on this relationship if you wish, applying your Buddhist studies, make it a task for yourself to learn to cope differently with the way she treats you over time, or you could just end it. You could wish her well and put that energy into other things and other people.'

I don't know what the other student made of this response, but it certainly struck a chord with me. I knew I had to end my best friendship. It wasn't serving either of us, and frankly I didn't see the benefit in applying myself to coping better with it. I didn't like the lady in question and she didn't like me. I decided to use my energy elsewhere, and I ended it.

I ended it very badly, I'm afraid to admit. I wasn't quite at the stage where I could meet with her to explain my decision, or even tell her over the phone. I'm ashamed to say, I didn't even text, email, send a carrier pigeon or make smoke signals from my bedroom window. I just ignored her. I unfriended her on Facebook, ignored her calls and deleted all evidence of her from my life. I stopped attending events I knew she'd be at, and eventually she and everyone else we knew got the message. She tried via various platforms to ask me if I was 'dumping' her, but I ignored her and eventually she stopped trying to communicate with me.

Yeah, I did it in the lowest, most hurtful, humiliating way possible, and I'm not proud of it. In my defence, I really believe that friendships are harder to end than romantic relationships. To a lot of people – by whom I again mean straight men – that's a completely ridiculous idea. I can't imagine my dad ever soul-searching about the influence his mates Reg and Billy were having on his self-esteem and personal growth. I don't remember him ever fretting that they might be talking about him if he couldn't make it to the pub one night. Straight male friendships seem to be pretty straight-forward to me, although I'm sure they are full of nuances I've missed.

For many of us, though, one single friendship rules our lives. It's a big influence to just leave unchecked and never question its value or consequences. We'll put up with a dysfunctional friendship way longer than we'll cop a bad boyfriend or girlfriend. Perhaps it's because the signs of a romance in trouble are easier to spot. Romantic problems are also exactly the kind of scenario where we rely on friends to help us sort out what's going on and what we need to do. When we do break up with a partner, it's our best friends who console us, keep us busy, get us drunk and make us laugh. We rely on them to get us through.

In the case of this friendship break-up, all my friends were her friends too, and while I'd certainly spent plenty of time discussing this woman's faults with our mutuals in the past, I didn't want to live that way anymore. That was the whole point. So I ended up isolating myself. I knew I was doing the right thing – but, wow, I think it was the loneliest time in my life.

I was sort of weirdly friendless for all intents and purposes for a couple of years after that. I mean, I fooled around with acquaintances, but nothing serious, you know? Eventually I started going out and seeing potential friends again, but I'm still BFF celibate. While I have women I love and upon whose counsel I rely when it comes to everything from work dramas to dealing with my children's head lice, I don't let myself get caught up in particular friendships. I don't let myself get attached and grasp for them, and you can bet I take off at a million miles an hour if I feel anyone grasping at me!

I am sitting comfortably next to these woman on that rollercoaster ride. We are experiencing the ups and downs together, and there is no clawing at each other, no screaming each other's names. This is love without Attachment – and if we can have it with friends, then there is no reason to think we can't have it in romance.

I've never looked back from ending that last frenemy-ship, and I have to tell you, neither has she! Thanks to our old pal the internet, I've kept tabs on her from afar over the years and I know she has absolutely soared. She has an exciting, international career in which she's appreciated and feted, and she's now married to a wonderful old friend. I'm very happy to see her doing well, and sometimes I'm tempted to contact her to tell her so. Then I wonder what the real purpose of that would be. What would be my intention? Intention is everything in Buddhism. Good deeds done with selfish intentions are still worthwhile, but nothing beats good deeds with good intentions. Would I be contacting her to offer congratulations, or would it be to ease my conscience after the way I treated her? Can it be both? Does one negate the other? I'm honestly not sure, and I don't know if I'm strong enough, even after all these years, not to fall back into that destructive friendship, so for now I'm letting it go.

American Buddhist nun Pema Chodron said, 'If we learn to open our hearts, anyone, including the people who drive us crazy, can be our teacher.'

We can learn from them from afar, though, if we're not strong enough yet to interact with them differently – unless of course they happen to the father of our children. That's the one relationship you can't ever cut off or leave behind, so I guess Adrian will continue 'teaching' me for the rest of my life. Best I continue working on how to make the most of it, I guess!

KEY POINTS

- There is nothing wrong with loving others, but craving them and grasping at them (Attachment) is unhealthy. It makes people pull away and it can never be satisfied.

- Attachment relies on the misunderstanding that things always stay the same. The antidote to this is Emptiness. Do you really want that person or thing? Approach again with Emptiness and see.

- Attachment is all about your fears. Only you can overcome them. If you are seeking relief in other people, you'll never be satisfied. Find relief in yourself and companionship in others.

- Attachment doesn't strengthen relationships; it erodes them, because we're always reacting to what we wish our partner was doing instead of what they are actually doing. The amount of angst in a relationship is a good indication of how much Attachment is going on.

- Friendships can be as prone to Attachment as romantic relationships.

- Other people have no power over our emotions. We choose how we react to them.

- Love without Attachment is possible. You are working on achieving it right now! In a relationship without Attachment, both people are able to enjoy the other's company without demanding more.

SELF-REFLECTION

- Think of a time recently when you lashed out at someone or something. Investigate your thoughts – what were you really attached to? What did you want to be happening that wasn't happening?

- Is there a troubling, attached relationship in your life that you can end? Why not end it?

- Is there a positive, non-attached relationship in your life from which you can draw inspiration?

- What are the positives to breaking up? Make your own checklist to help you talk yourself out of Attachment reactions.

4

Mindfulness

Mindfulness is without a doubt one of the most overused buzzwords of recent times – right up there with 'viral', 'hack', 'disruptive', 'intuitive', 'sustainable', 'transparent', 'robust', 'proactive' and 'authentic'. These are the words that launched a thousand TED Talks and were immediately integrated into the lexicons of obedient but unimaginative corporate types, to rebrand everything from warfare to toothpaste. ('Rebrand' is another one.) They are frequently applied to things that have nothing to do with their original meaning.

Colouring for mindfulness is a perfect example. Someone somewhere has invented an entirely new market by using the word 'mindfulness' to persuade adults – let's be honest, adult women – that there's a higher purpose, even a spirituality, to colouring. Brilliant!

The problem is that while colouring is relaxing and gently hypnotic, it's no more mindful than doing the dishes or watching the cricket. You're just escaping your thoughts. True mindfulness is remaining completely present with your thoughts and really dealing with them.

Cracking open a nice new colouring book and a pack of twenty-five Derwents might help you calm down after an upsetting break-up-related incident, but mindfulness will help you identify what upset you in the first place. Once you've done that, you can work on strategies to protect yourself from those triggers. You can become emotionally bulletproof! Colouring can't give you that.

Mindfulness is too important, too wonderful and too powerful for us to let it become diluted as a well-marketed fad. It is the key to unlocking Buddhist philosophy and creating tangible changes in you life. So let's explore what it really is.

I once read an article that defined mindfulness as 'the intentional, non-judgemental awareness of moment-to-moment experience'. While that definition is a bit clinical, it does highlight that mindfulness is a kind of scientific investigation of our own feelings and motivations. In mindfulness, we're trying to calmly observe the emotional response in the moment and approach it logically. We then want to be able to let that moment go and live completely in the next moment.

Let's look at an example.

Recently I bought a salad sandwich and a banana at the airport. I put them on the counter and asked for a coffee too.

'That'll be $24,' said the the woman at the register.

> **MINDFULNESS** placing your attention on the present moment

'Oh I'm just paying for the sandwich, the banana and the coffee,' I said, thinking she'd confused my order with someone else's.

'Yes,' she yelled, 'this is the airport and that's how much it costs – do you want it or not?!'

Yowser!

How can we interpret this situation? One way of looking at it is that the server was being needlessly rude to me, deliberately humiliating me in front of other people – and I was being ripped off for a sandwich into the bargain!

If I used this interpretation, I might react by being rude right back at her in retaliation. I might make a big song and dance about it and try to embarrass her. I might throw the damn sandwich at her and tell her to forget it. Or ask to see her manager to complain! But whatever happens from there, it won't end well. At the very least I'll be grumpy and hungry for the rest of the afternoon – and I don't want to be grumpy and hungry. I want to be peaceful, damn it!

So here's another way of dealing with it. If I give myself a moment to collect my thoughts in the second after she's yelled in my face, I can quickly brush the situation off as having no real relevance to me or my day. That's her trip, basically, and not my problem. Obviously people complain about the prices in the cafe all the time and she's sick of it, but I didn't know that and there's nothing I can do about it, except not upset her further. I don't have to assign any opinions to the situation, or activate any defensive tactics. For all I know, annoying customers might be the least of her problems that day. Whatever she's got going on has nothing to do with me unless I let it upset me too, and that would be a dumb thing to do, wouldn't it?

Instead of thinking to myself, 'What a moll. Who does she think she is? She can't talk to me that way and

I'm going to let her know!' I could think to myself, 'Wow, something's bothering that lady. Poor thing. Right, have I got everything? How long until my flight? What's next?'

If I can let the incident pass me by without any emotional involvement – and without judgement as to whether the encounter was good or bad – I've succeeded in maintaining my own peace through mindfulness.

Okay, so I'm sure we all feel great about that pretty benign example, but let's bring it back to the reactionary minefield of break-ups.

There was a period of time after Adrian and I decided to divorce and move away from each other, but before we actually had, when he suddenly stopped speaking to me. We'd been getting along well, and had both been focusing on trying to make the move sound exciting for the sake of the kids. On top of that, I'd agreed to a settlement that I thought was very generous to Adrian, so, yeah, I thought I deserved a bit of friendliness. What I got was grunts of acknowledgement and no eye contact. It really pushed all my old panic buttons.

My instinct was to demand that Adrian treat me differently. I wanted to march into his home and list off all the reasons he owed me gratitude, love and respect, and to insist he bloody gave them to me immediately! That is definitely what I would have done a year earlier, before I'd committed to using Buddhist principles to work though the break-up.

The battle about Adrian not treating me as I believed I deserved to be treated was in our past and we'd fought it many times without it ever ending well. By staying mindful I was able to remember that important fact and stop myself from going back there. In the flurry of thoughts that went through my mind, in that instant I realised he was ignoring me, I was able to grab onto the one that said, 'Don't engage!'

The hours I would previously have spent fighting with him, were instead spent in quiet contemplation. The more I thought about it, the more I believed he was probably freaking out about moving. He's never liked it, and he was probably just having a bit of a wobble about the massive changes happening in his life. I'm sure he was feeling fear about the future, anger towards me for my part in the break-down of our marriage, and sadness at the idea of not seeing the kids every day. But for the first time in our relationship, I accepted that whatever had his knickers in a twist, it was nothing to do with me.

Within minutes, I'd put it out of my mind – like, all the way out. I didn't stew on it or cry, or let it get to me in any way. I just stopped thinking about it and moved on to something else. Mind you, I did take a little break to congratulate myself. It was a really momentous behavioural shift for me, and I was thrilled about it. It was one of those moments that made me feel like it was going to be all right. Like *I* was going to be all right.

Adrian was no more responsible for my mood and feelings that night than the lady in the shop was. In the end, I am responsible for my emotions, and I choose to feel happy, no matter how many rude jerks there are in the world.

I know we can feel helpless about our reactions sometimes, especially when dealing with people who really know how to press our buttons and fire us up, like ex partners. Undisciplined reactions can strike like lightening, and before you know it you've said or done something you'll live to regret. 'I couldn't help myself!' we'll say later after some kind of disastrous blow-up, but the science says that by telling ourselves over and over to respond differently to a particular stimulus, like relationship dramas, we really can change the way we react to it. I'm no neuroscientist or meditation master, but I am a person who's changed the way I react to particular situations – quite incredibly, if I do say so myself. So much so that I know for a fact my more recent colleagues and those I worked with a decade ago use very different lists of adjectives to describe my personality! It would definitely sound like they were describing two different people. Unfortunately, I took a lot longer to discipline myself at home.

I got there eventually, although too late for our marriage, but even Adrian will admit that my attitude and outlook are much calmer these days. He often tells me how relieved he is that I haven't freaked out like he thought I would about something or other. It's our partners who bear the brunt of our mindless emotional chaos. We vent our frustrations at home because we'd never dream of doing it at work, but when home is the problem, venting becomes arguing and it just multiplies endlessly.

One of the benefits of breaking up is that it's made me emotionally self-sufficient. I used to rely heavily on Adrian to soothe me, but when my issues with him became my major problem I had to learn to soothe myself. Mindfulness is the key.

Let's look at how you can get some of that mindful goodness working in *your* life.

Meditation is really where it's at when it comes to making mindfulness a habit, but I know it can seem pretty hardcore and scary. When I mentioned science earlier, I was referring to studies that show that by meditating on things we are more likely to remember and incorporate them into the rest of our day. What we're talking about here is neuroplasticity – the process by which the brain reorganises itself in response to it's environment. The idea is the more we tell our brains to react in a certain way, the more likely it is to adopt that response as instinctive.

If we meditate on mindfulness, we'll become more mindful during the rest of the day when we're not meditating. The more we focus on peacefulness, the more peaceful we'll become, and so on. When we change our thoughts, we change our reactions – then we change our reality.

So how do you actually meditate?

Well, the first thing you have to do is find a peaceful place to sit. It doesn't have to be silent, which is lucky, because I can't think of a single silent place within a hundred-kilometre radius of my place. It just needs to be somewhere comfortable, where no-one will actively try to distract you. If you're anything like me, the alert noise of an email arriving on your computer or phone is enough to distract you, so switch off or mute all electronics. If you're listening to a guided meditation on your phone, be sure to switch it to flight mode, because you can back it in that every man and his dog plus a few long-lost cousins and telemarketers will decide to call, email and text you during those couple of minutes.

I like to burn incense while I meditate, if possible. It helps me set the mood, and creates a sense memory that settles me down faster over time. It also lends an air of ceremony and ritual to the occasion, which I like (no doubt a throwback to my Catholic childhood).

Once you're settled and comfortable, commence breathing! Obviously you've been breathing all along, but now become aware of your breathing. Listen to your breath, and feel it. If you're doing a guided meditation, the recording will instruct you to take some deep breaths, but you'll probably feel like doing this anyway, because we seem to respect and enjoy breathing more when we concentrate on hearing and feeling it.

Tap into how your body moves as the breath moves in and out. Does your chest rise? Does your belly expand? Where does it go? Which bit of your body deflates first? Keep listening and following the breath as it flows into and out of your body like a tide. Feel it where it enters your body through your nostrils, and how it flows over your lips when it exits. This practice is often referred to as 'returning to the breath', and it's your meditation home base. Whenever you feel yourself drifting away with a thought, or even falling asleep, return to your breath – concentrate on feeling it and hearing it again.

Thoughts will enter your mind constantly at first. Even thoughts of how the meditation is going will distract you from the actual meditation. Don't panic: this is quite natural. Acknowledge every thought as it drifts into your mind, and then send it out again. Your internal monologue might sound something like this: 'Oh, I've just remembered my ex's phone is still in my name. Okay, I'll deal with that later, out you go,' and back to the breath. 'Oh wow, I think I'm meditating properly, but now I'm not because I'm thinking about it. Okay, I'll just get back to it then,' and back to the breath. 'Pa pa pa poker face, pa pa poker face, ma ma ma ma, oh no, I'm singing Lady Gaga's 'Poker Face' in my mind instead of meditating. Out you go, Lady Gaga,' and back to the breath.

Over time, the spaces of meditation between the distracting thoughts will grow longer and Lady Gaga's greatest hits will feature less prominently – at least that's how it went for me.

Quieting our own mental pollution is one level, but the next level is allowing actual physical distractions to pass us by without distracting us. Barking dogs, noisy neighbours, squabbling children in the next room, whatever the disturbance is, our aim is to acknowledge it like we would a random thought, but not form a judgement about it. Not let it get to us, in other words.

Your normal reaction might be to scream at the kids to stop fighting and cork their gobs because you don't ask for much in this world and you can't even get a couple of minutes' peace in your own bloody home, and no-one's going to Maccas later if they don't knock it off! The task during meditation is to simply acknowledge the noise coming from the other room, without making a sound or moving an inch, and then take your attention back to your breath. We want to learn to simply witness things as they arise and then let them fall away.

As you improve at this exercise, you'll get better at simply witnessing things in your daily life and letting them fall away without getting emotionally involved. That is real mindfulness.

Imagine being able to simply witness your ex-partner's behaviour, without having any feelings about it. Imagine just witnessing your parents' intrusive questions, your married friends' pity and your frenemies' delight and then being able to get on with your day, completely emotionally free. Now, that's worth working for, isn't it?

Good, because meditation is hard. Lots of people give up because they can't 'get it', but I think most of us spend most of our time not getting it. Guided meditation is an excellent way to start and is in no way 'cheating'. His Holiness the Dalai Lama always says it's better to meditate for five minutes a day than not at all and I'm confident he'd rubber-stamp a five-minute guided meditation if it helped us develop a regular, consistent practice.

Don't give up after your first failure. Keep setting your intention every morning, keep trying to slow down your reactions and give yourself a moment to think about what's really going on inside your head, and keep meditating.

If finding a peaceful space to meditate is hard for you, like it is for me, improvise. Meditation classes are fantastic, but if you can't find the time for that, the car can be a good spot. I find a quiet place on my commute to or from work, like at a park or the beach, and I play a five-minute guided meditation for myself. I have a tendency to fall asleep when I meditate by myself, which is another reason to use a guided meditation. They usually end with bells or other noises to help wake you up.

Mindfulness is not just about keeping you in a good mood, it's also very important to the practical day-to-day running of your life, and to your mental health. Vietnamese monk Thich Nhat Hanh is one of my favourite Buddhist authors and teachers. He describes the importance of mindfulness this way: 'Our true home is not in the past. Our true home is not in the future. Our true home is in the here and the now. Life is available only in the here and the now, and it is our true home.'

The here and now is where your life is actually happening. The past is done and you can have no further impact on it. The future is full of unknowns and you can't guess at the influences your life will fall under, even one minute from now, that will change your course. There's that old saying: 'If you want to make God laugh, tell him your plans.' Anyone who has small children knows how easily and quickly the best-laid plans can be derailed. There are any number of unknowns we need to work around every day that we can't blame on anyone. From flat tyres to major illnesses, our futures are full of things we can't possibly plan for. In fact, that is the only prediction we can make with certainty.

There are lots of problems with focusing on the future. When we over-plan a future event or moment, we run the risk of freaking out if it doesn't work out the way we envisioned it. We can get so caught up in planning that we never actually get around to doing anything, and we can miss out on opportunities that pop up along the way because they don't fit in with our plan (the plan may never actually eventuate anyway, because life's like that).

Obviously we need to forward-plan some elements of our lives. I'm not suggesting you walk out of the house naked, torch your ex's car and spend all your money on a Prada handbag because it feels good in the moment. Considering the likely consequences of our actions in advance makes sense, as does working to create a comfortable future for ourselves and our families. What doesn't make sense is ignoring the here and now in favour of daydreaming or stressing about the future.

Similarly, we need to review our past and take stock, particularly after a relationship breakdown. We need to be honest with ourselves about our mistakes and also about the kinds of patterns we don't want to repeat. But we don't want to obsess over every last detail, running it over and over in our minds, or never trust anyone again, or fantasise about reclaiming our old life. None of that will lead to happiness or peace.

If I am depressed, I am living in the past.
If I am anxious, I am living in the future.

UNKNOWN

There are two alarm bells in our brains that will alert us when we stray dangerously from mindfulness – depression and anxiety. Our task is to stop ignoring them and stop self-medicating to deal with them.

When I feel depressed, I ask myself what I'm depressed about. Most of the time I'm feeling embarrassed about or obsessing over something I've done or said. Invariably, I'm focusing on something in the past that I can't change – something that keeps me completely distracted and disconnected from the present. I remind myself to snap out of it and get with the present, because the past is a road to nowhere.

I take the same approach when I'm feeling anxious. Most of the time when I feel anxious, it's because I'm worried about something in the future. I'm scared I'm not going to get a job I want, or that I won't be very good at something, or that I'm going to have a horrible week because I've booked too many things into it and there'll be no time to rest. Obviously fretting about it doesn't help, it just makes it harder to cope with the present and it makes me irritable, which causes me problems with other people.

For me, depression and anxiety have become indicators that I'm not living in the present and I'm not living mindfully. Coming to terms with the fact that my husband no longer loved me was, naturally, depressing. I constantly looked back to a time in my life when he did love me. I craved that time, mourned its passing and blamed him for my depression. The idea of a life without his affection made me very anxious. I would lie awake at night formulating frightening scenarios of the future in my mind and wondering how on earth I'd deal with them without him. What if I spent the rest of my life alone, or worse, what if I brought a man into our lives who hurt one or all of us? What if my kids ended up with a step-parent they hated? What if I couldn't cope with raising my children alone?

What it? What if? *What if?*

In order to deal with depression and anxiety as they arose, I had to develop a new habit – taking a moment to collect my thoughts. It really is just about not reacting straight away. Even if I feel it looks silly, I'll wait for a couple of seconds, sometimes in mid-conversation, and just run through what I'm really feeling. By doing this, I can stop myself reacting in a way that I'll regret. If someone says something rude to me, for example, I'll take a few moments to process it and make a decision about what to say or do next, rather than just lash out with the first thing that comes to mind. In doing so, I might realise I'm taking it the wrong way, or that the other person doesn't know the critical detail that makes what they've said rude. More often than not, I'll realise that the negative reaction I was about to have was unwarranted and unnecessary.

Of course sometimes it's not, though. Sometimes I find myself in conversation with a total jerk I want to verbally pulverise! In that situation I'll sometimes decide to remove myself, and I'll say: 'Look, I'm actually going to remove myself right now because I don't want to do or say something I'll regret. I'll talk to you about this later.'

The habit of thought collection, which is just a quick stocktake of what's really going on when you feel your heart rate quicken and your eyes twitch, will change your life. Honestly, you won't believe how much drama it will remove. Just think about how many times you look back on a situation and wish you'd handled it differently. Then imagine having that thought in the actual moment, before you commit to a reaction. Thought collection before reaction is mindfulness in action.

Here's an example. While Adrian and I were still living on the same premises – me in the house and he in the granny flat – I heard on the grapevine that Adrian had been contacting a woman we both know. I'd always thought she was his type – she was like a younger, more carefree version of me – but I was shocked that he was already considering seeing someone else. Whether he was actually interested in a relationship with her or not I don't know, but I'm sure you can imagine what my initial reaction to this news was. It was a real test for me: of course I was jealous and hurt, and depression and anxiety both made an appearance in the minutes after I heard the news.

I fantasised briefly about reacting in ways that would definitely have had negative consequences. I considered swaggering into his place and letting him know I knew, just as a power play, to embarrass him, make him feel pathetic and make out that I'm all-seeing and all-knowing. I wanted to warn him against partying with women around my kids. I knew he wouldn't do that, but I was prepared to pretend I was worried about it. My first instincts were to be a real bitch.

Instead, I took some time and collected my thoughts.

I lay in my bed, looking at the ceiling, breathing deeply, thinking. I focused on the fact that Adrian and I were getting along really well. If I gave him a hard time about this other woman it would finish that and destroy any trust we'd built as friends. I reminded myself that he was well within his rights to get out there and get among it, and he hadn't actually done anything wrong. I told myself over and over that this was an excellent opportunity to practise, and that if I could handle such news this first time, it would never hurt as much again.

Adrian strolled into my place a little later, excitedly telling the kids about some new Lego he had waiting for them at his place. As he waffled on at my kitchen bench, I bit my tongue. I wanted to launch at him so badly, but I didn't. I kept reminding myself of all the reasons why it was best to pretend I knew nothing. As the day wore on, and the kids came and went happily between the houses,

I struggled less and less with it. By the time I bathed them, put them in their jim-jams and sent them to his place for bed, I was completely at peace. I enjoyed a quiet night alone with a glass of wine and my wonderful new life partner, Netflix. That could have been a very different day for all of us. That day was mindfulness at work.

Speaking of glasses of wine, substances are other warning signs worth paying attention to.

Self-medication has been a problem for me in the past. Now I know that if I'm looking for a glass of wine on a weeknight, something's up. I'm not saying that's a sign for everyone, and I know it may sound a bit alarmist, but for me it's definitely a sign that something's out of balance. When I'm relaxed about life, I don't think about drinking much. It's not really my thing. As a younger woman, though, at various times I resorted to amphetamines, pills, pot and heroin to cope with depression and anxiety. I'd never heard of self-medicating back then, or even the idea that alcohol and drug abuse can be a sign of someone struggling with mental illness. I thought I was having fun and being cool, but at a certain point I realised I was neither and that my use of these substances was a way of trying to cope with distressing emotions.

Are you turning to something to distract yourself from the pain of your break-up? You might want to look into that and reach out for help if it's a problem for you. A clear head is crucial to pulling yourself back together after a break-up.

Typically, break-ups stir up a lot of regret about the past and a lot of fear of the future. That is completely normal and I can't snap my fingers and make it go away for you. I can, however, encourage you towards some self-care that'll put you on the road to recovery. It starts with living in the moment you are actually living in.

The hardest part for me was stopping myself thinking about the happy times of my marriage and remembering moments when I felt loved and confident. Those memories were like daggers to my heart and could set me right back to the beginning of the recovery process. I had to be very stern with myself when one of those memories popped into my head. I had to shut it down immediately and refocus on the present. As time went by, I was able to enjoy those memories again, as long as I remained mindful and honest about the feelings they produced.

KEY POINTS

- Mindfulness is placing your attention on the present. It helps us to become aware of our real feelings and motivations and to operate in the world with a clear mind, unclouded by past issues or fears for the future.

- Break-ups make us feel as though our life as we know it is over, which is fertile ground for chaotic swinging between past and future thinking. Mindfulness brings us back to the present.

- Break-ups are full of reflexive emotional reactions. Mindfulness gives us a minute to decide upon how we want to react, which helps us avoid disastrous deeds. When we change our reactions, we change our reality.

- Meditation helps make mindfulness a habit. Even five minutes of meditation a day is beneficial.

- Planning and reviewing are reasonable and helpful things to do in life, but obsessing over the past and future while ignoring the present is not. Apply some discipline to examining what went wrong in a relationship and what sort of future you want for yourself.

SELF-REFLECTION

- How could you build some mindfulness into your day?
  Think about how you could establish a meditation
  practice – even just five minutes a day.

- Are you feeling depressed or anxious? If you're
  depressed, you're living in the past.* If you're anxious,
  you're living in the future.

- Are you self-medicating? Care for yourself and ask for help
  if you need it.

*It should be noted that in this context, we're talking about situational
depression, that is, depression that's caused by something, as opposed to
clinical depression, which occurs without any apparent trauma or stressful
events present. Don't take your mental health lightly. Seek a professional
opinion if you feel it's out of your control.

5

Disturbing Emotions

'Disturbing' is such a great word, isn't it? There were definitely times during the last years of my marriage when I felt disturbed. Disturbed, insane, pathetic and unrecognisable – among many other things. I smashed stuff, cut myself, and crashed a car deliberately. I abandoned Adrian in a Thai airport, slapped him in a Brisbane bar and cried to a stranger on a German train. As a wise man once said: I've done all the dumb things.

According to Buddha, the way to deal with disturbing actions once and for all is to deal with the emotions that produce them.

Disturbing emotions aren't hard to identify. They're things like anger, greed, jealousy, hate, pride, delusion and bitterness.

I think of them as the shallow, defensive emotions that charge out in front of us, protecting our deeper, more vulnerable feelings. For instance, I have a very deep-seated fear of rejection, and when Adrian seems to be ignoring me I often react with anger and resentment. React-ing angrily helps me keep the painful feeling of rejection hidden and avoid dealing with it. It also causes big, ugly fights in which a million other contentious issues are raised and more often than not one or both of us ends up doing something dumb and regrettable, sometimes in a foreign country.

DISTURBING EMOTIONS defensive emotions that erupt out of us when we are challenged

The *Great Tibetan Dictionary* (*Bod kyi tshig mdzod chen mo*) defines disturbing emotions as 'mental events that incite one to unvirtuous actions and cause one's being to be very unpeaceful'.

So disturbing emotions are things that happen in our own minds (mental events) which make us act like idiots (incite us to unvirtuous actions) and create problems for us (cause our being to be unpeaceful).

To work backwards, our problems are generally caused by our actions and/or reactions to our emotions, not to anyone else's actions. Our emotions are *our* responsibility. When we learn to control our emotions, it follows that we can control our actions and therefore cease to create problems for ourselves.

That's a pretty revolutionary leap of logic if you think about it. We normally try to stop feeling bad because it feels bad, and leave it at that. But Buddha's main concern with disturbing emotions is that our feelings create bad behaviour and cause us unpeacefulness.

As far as Buddha is concerned, the end game is not happiness, but *peacefulness*. This distinction is important. As my ex-husband and I navigated the tricky seas of our break-up, I found I could be *at peace* with certain agreements we made through mediation, even if they didn't exactly make me *happy*.

Happiness has some drawbacks: it can easily give way to greed. What makes me happy today may not feel like enough tomorrow. Peace is more enduring. It is about acceptance. I'm not exactly happy about elements of our settlement, but I accept the compromises as the price of moving on independently and I'm at peace with them.

Peace is the number one goal of the Buddhist. It's not a selfish goal, because it's believed that a peaceful person can be of greater service to others. As we know, Buddha believed we are all connected, so our emotional discipline and peacefulness is of great benefit to the world. Every day I see the direct effect my peacefulness, or lack thereof, has on my children's world. Unlike adults, when I am acting out my disturbing emotions they aren't content to simply avoid me and complain about my bad behaviour behind my back. When I'm unpeaceful it's written all over their sad little faces, and it's horrible.

Properly dealing with disturbing emotions isn't about trying to forget about them or painting on a fake smile; it's about being honest with ourselves, disciplined in our approach and taking responsibility for our own emotions. It's hard work, but if you're ready for the challenge it'll make a big difference in every aspect of your life.

The most obvious disturbing emotions involved in break-ups are anger, jealousy and pride. Let's tackle them one by one.

ANGER

Buddha believed our emotions were our business. He taught that no-one else can control them. Other people don't *make* us angry, we *react angrily* to their behaviour. Therefore, we can choose to react differently.

If ever there's someone you might be prone to accusing of making you feel miserable, it's an ex-partner. After all, didn't you once credit him or her with making you happy? So why not assume they have also made you miserable? Well, one unknown genius put it this way: 'Holding onto anger is like drinking poison and expecting the other person to die.'

The most important reason to take responsibility for and control of your anger is that it hurts *you*, not them. It hurts you a lot, so don't just hope and pray someone else will take this feeling away for you. You have to do it yourself.

Look very deeply inside yourself to see if your anger has actually been serving you in some way. Have you been using it to bully other people? Did your ex-partner give in to you when you became angry? Do your kids creep around trying to make you happy when you're angry? Did your parents reward your anger by giving in to your demands? You may have developed a habit of leaping to and holding on to anger because it seems to work for you. But I promise you, in the long term it doesn't.

I'm embarrassed to admit it, but I was guilty of using anger to control my husband. It worked for a while, in that he responded with affection and attention. He stopped reacting that way eventually though, and it became one of the biggest problems in our marriage. Not only did he stop trying to alleviate my anger for me, he reached the point where he couldn't care less if I was angry or not and he certainly didn't hesitate to behave in ways that were guaranteed to spark my fury. I'd go so far as to say sometimes he clearly enjoyed waving the red rag at my bullish temper.

Adrian began breaking agreements we'd made about child care. He started inviting friends over for all-night drinking and Xbox sessions when I had to get up at 4.30 a.m. the next day for work. He ignored text messages and phone calls. All of this was very out of character, even for an impermanent being who was still arising! Tellingly, he stopped doing all of these things again when we decided to divorce. Funny that!

In retrospect, I think Adrian 'making' me angry was one of the ways in which he was trying to tell me things had changed. He had changed, and my old ways of dealing with him weren't going to cut it anymore.

In a selfish, practical sense, I can see now how vulnerable my anger made me. There I was, thinking I was ten feet tall, stomping around, threatening to get angry, like that was really powerful, but actually I might as well have given

Adrian a red hot stick with which to poke me whenever I was annoying him.

No matter how warranted my anger over his behaviour seemed, it still created suffering for me and my children, which is exactly what I didn't want. After years of tearing my hair out over escalating fights, I finally realised what I had to do.

I made a decision to stop being an angry person. Not just to control my anger, but to stop it completely. It was a really big decision to make, because I didn't know if it was possible, and I worried about how I'd defend myself in this world without it.

The reasons to be angry didn't stop coming, but I stopped reacting to them with anger. I wrote earlier of a rush of thoughts flooding my mind in a difficult moment, and of mindfulness allowing me to reach out and choose the one that said 'DON'T ENGAGE!' The rest of my options in that moment were all based on anger and I flatly refused to grab them.

My friend Adam Richard once said to me of his own mellowing, 'It's like there's a drop-down menu in my mind. There are lots of horrible things I can choose to say and do, and in the past I would have, but increasingly I choose a positive option.'

We often blame others for making us mad or breaking our hearts. We go with those disturbing emotions because we think we have no choice. We might feel hatred for them and for what *they've done to us*. I once told another friend, Lawrence Mooney, that I hated someone. I'll never forget how he responded: 'When you hate someone, you are their prisoner.'

Did he make that up? I don't know, but I've lived by it ever since. What's the use in dedicating time and energy to hating Adrian because he doesn't love me anymore? I can free myself. I can choose peace.

If you're still unsure about whether or not you have a problem with anger, consider the example of a bloke I used to know called Dave McGuire. He was a friend of my parents when I was a kid. Due to his crazy temper, everyone called him 'Mad Dog'. You'd think once you obtained a nickname like Mad Dog you might sit down and have a bit of a think about how you're going with life, but not Dave. Dave was convinced he was a victim of his surroundings – all of his surroundings, all the time.

He had a neighbour who decided he'd mow the lawn bright and early every Sunday morning, which was coincidentally Dave's only chance at a sleep-in all week. On the first Sunday he asked the neighbour nicely if he could stop mowing; on the second Sunday he yelled out the window. On the third Sunday he stormed next door in his boxer shorts and threw the neighbour's lawn mower in the pool.

Not only did Dave have to pay for a new mower, but his now antagonistic neighbour continued his Sunday mows, threatening to call the police if Dave ever made a peep about it again. Let's just say that Dave's temper had brought him to the attention of the police before, so he was in no position to argue.

Some of Dave's tantrums cost him a little – like the time he jumped up and down on his own lunchbox because it wouldn't close – and some cost him a lot – like the time he repeatedly rammed his ute into the front wall of his house because he couldn't get the automatic garage door to work. One thing was certain; Dave's anger always cost him.

Dave's biggest problem was that he truly believed other people were at fault. He blamed his wife for buying him a cheap lunchbox, his kids for playing with the garage opener until the batteries ran flat, and his neighbour for being an inconsiderate, obnoxious jerk. In some ways he was right – his wife did buy the lunchbox, his kids did run the batteries down and his neighbour did mow early in the morning – but it was his anger that turned these facts into major disasters.

Imagine if Dave had thrown that lunchbox away and chosen a new one for himself at the shops, instead of jumping on it and becoming a laughing stock on the building site. Imagine if he'd left the ute in the driveway and gone inside to replace the batteries, while giving the kids a bit of a stern talking to about playing with the garage door opener, instead of smashing his own house and scaring them half to death. Can you imagine how terrified they must have been? How that and other episodes must have tainted their relationship with their dad?

Of course someone mowing the lawn while you're trying to sleep is incredibly annoying, but can you imagine how much worse it would have been afterwards, when the neighbour continued his early-morning mows after the pool incident?

The story of Mad Dog McGuire is easy to grasp. He was a guy who refused to accept his own part in his troubles. His sense of entitlement to everything from a silent neighbourhood on Sunday mornings to an idiot-proof lunchbox is obviously obnoxious as hell, as is his firm conviction that he is the only person within coo-ee with a brain in his head.

You may not be as bad as Mad Dog, but ask yourself this: how often have you thought to yourself something like, 'I'm surrounded by idiots!' 'Am I the only one working around here?' 'Why can't anyone drive today?' or 'My God, you're useless!' How often do you unleash your inner Mad Dog?

It's easy for us to judge other people's anger issues, especially when they're so flamboyant, but our own underlying anger can be an insidiously destructive force. Both Adrian and I realised through counselling that we harboured anger towards our parents over certain things. When we accidentally reminded each other of our parents there was hell to pay, often leaving the offending partner with no idea what had happened or why.

Sometimes we harboured anger at each other that bubbled away just under the surface, looking for an outlet. We both thought we were doing the right thing by not airing every little grievance because we were trying to avoid arguments, but instead of finding ways to deal with those issues, we stewed over them until we lost our composure over something else and then let it all out in a huge bonfire of resentment.

Can you relate to that? From what I can gather after many hours of conversations with female friends, volcanos of simmering anger sitting just below the surface of a marriage are not uncommon.

This is where our old pal mindfulness comes back into play. When we've blown up over something minor, our task is to look deep within ourselves to find out why. Why do I sometimes get so angry about such little things? There is always a reason, but without knowing or accepting what it really is, we're just shadow boxing, and probably injuring a few innocent bystanders whom we happen to love very much.

When we feel anger flaring, no matter how justified we believe it is right then and there, we need to take that moment to collect our thoughts. Just walk away, Renee! Seriously, walk away. Even if you don't experience a life-changing epiphany, you'll have changed the course of that particular situation, and quite possibly prevented yourself from doing something you'll be ashamed of later.

The antidote to anger is patience. It takes a lot of patience to turn down the opportunity to yell and swear and break stuff when you're living through a stressful, frustrating time like a break-up. Especially when someone has given you a golden opportunity to cut loose. Really letting rip with an angry tantrum relieves a shit-ton of pent-up emotion: fact!

The trouble is that it doesn't change the causes of the anger and you'll have to live with the consequences.

A patient response will give you an enormous feeling of achievement and, dare I say, pride (not always a bad thing). It will give you clarity. The patient response gave me the space to recognise my marriage needed to end. It wasn't a bad patch, we weren't going through a phase, and there was no way of fixing it. Frankly, my husband wanted out and the more I tried to accommodate him, punish him and implement new strategies, the more extreme his rebellion became.

A patient response to his behaviour helped me look at it clinically, sort of from a distance. I could see it wasn't making him happy either; he was scrambling, trying to change things any way he could because he was so unhappy with the way things were. My patience sort of slowed everything down, and gave me the opportunity to inject some compassion into my perspective. I still loved Adrian very much, and I could see he was drowning. The more I grasped for him, the further I pushed him under.

There's an old saying: 'If you love someone, set them free. If they come back they're yours, if they don't they never were.' Patience helped me remember that, from a Buddhist perspective, Adrian is not mine and never was. I was just lucky enough to get to walk beside him for a while, but that walk is over, and no amount of dragging or carrying or coaxing him along is going to change that. It is what it is, so what's the point in getting mad and walking around with puffy eyes all the time?

So how do you become patient? Well, it takes patience! Like so many other things we're taking about in this book, we have to keep reminding ourselves that we want to do it, and forgive ourselves when we fail. This is a good intention to set yourself every morning: 'Today I will be more patient.' This will help you remember to be patient later when you need to be.

Try cultivating patience when you're not angry, by letting a car into your lane in traffic perhaps, or by assuring an elderly person struggling with the ticket machine in front of you that there's no hurry. If you have children, you'll have plenty of opportunities to practise patience. In this way you'll feel the satisfaction and peace that come with patience and you'll start to look for more opportunities to practise it. You may not believe me, but try it and see. Impatience is one of my greatest failings and even I get better at it with practice.

Here's the most interesting benefit I've found in refusing to be an angry person, it actually makes you seem really strong. Staying calm in infuriating situations impresses people so much, it makes you seem like a superhero! I was so worried I'd be left helpless without anger, but I actually feel more powerful than ever.

JEALOUSY

Jealousy is one of the least confessed to and most powerful of all the disturbing emotions. Jealousy is obviously a clear case of Attachment; it's grasping for something that someone else has and hating them for having it.

We often admit to acting out of anger: 'Sorry I yelled at you, I was just so angry!' But rarely do we cop to jealousy, because it's so embarrassing! When we're accused of jealousy, our impulse is to defend ourselves: 'As if I'm jealous that my ex has a new partner and I don't. No way!!'

The embarrassment factor was definitely part of the reason I didn't bail Adrian up immediately about his communications with our mutual female friend. During my deliberations about what to do, I realised I'd probably end up looking and feeling like a jealous idiot if I brought it up.

I spoke about jealousy with American comedian Marc Maron in a podcast once. He put it this way: 'It's very hard to get past the idea that their success is an indicator of your failure. It's a problem, but it's not their problem. It's something within yourself that needs to be reckoned with.' Deliberately or not, Maron has demonstrated there a profound understanding of the Buddha's teaching on disturbing emotions. He's come to understand that his feelings, including his sense of success and failure, are his own. No-one else puts them into his mind; he allows them to manifest there and only he can 'reckon' with them.

That conversation was about professional jealousy, which I've suffered from for most of my life, as do most comedians. In fact, I sometimes think that jealousy might be an appropriate collective noun for comedians: 'a flock of sheep', 'a swarm of flies', 'a jealousy of comedians'.

Some years back, I learnt a very effective method for dealing with my jealousy of other comedians – voicing it aloud. I have lots of very talented friends and they are constantly telling me about exciting opportunities that come their way. In the past I would fight to control my face as I seethed inside while they described these developments. I would then complain behind their backs about the unfairness of it all, and about how they didn't deserve it (and of course I did!). I may have struggled to have a positive thought about them for months. These days, I look them in the eye and say, 'I am so jealous!'

The admission of jealousy does two things. First, it acts as a massive compliment for the other person, which is exactly what they deserve in that moment. Second, it somehow releases me from the disturbing emotion. The great thing about jealousy is that while it feels powerful, it seems to dissipate relatively easily, just by acknowledging that it's there.

It took me a couple of days, but eventually I admitted to Adrian that I knew he'd been talking with another woman. I admitted that I'd felt jealousy when I first heard about it, but that I'd been able to work through that and was feeling okay about it all. He was shocked, to say the least, but ultimately relieved, and it went a long way to cementing our post-relationship relationship.

An ex-partner's new relationship is just the kind of anxious, future-thinking vortex that jealousy can trap us in if we let it. It can create it's own imaginary world to keep us very busy, while our real lives in the here and now struggle on without direction or discipline. Next thing we know, our actual lives are a chaotic mess because we've been investing everything we have into dealing with a fantasy future world that may never come to pass.

If you're struggling to overcome jealousy of your ex-partner, take some practical steps. Stop paying attention to what they're doing. Mute them on social media, stop asking people about them and avoid people who love telling you whether you ask or not. Take responsibility and take control. Your ex certainly isn't going to start screwing up their life just to make you feel better. Take it as motivation and get stuck in to your own life!

It comes back to peace versus happiness. We all need to find a way to accept that our ex-partner's life actually has nothing to do with us anymore. Of course if you share children you need to know the environment is safe for them, but when it comes to who your ex is sleeping with and how that's working out for them, how much money they're making in that new job or how great they look since leaving you, you don't have to be happy about it, but you have to *find peace* with it.

Buddha suggested a very specific, long-term antidote to jealousy. It's called 'unselfish joy': genuine, heartfelt happiness at the prosperity of others.

Imagine how great you feel when the person you love most in the world gets great news. Now imagine feeling that way when someone you don't like gets great news. Then imagine feeling that way when someone you don't even know gets that news. When you can feel equally joyous for all of them, BOOM! You're practising unselfish joy, baby!

Buddha was well aware that achieving unselfish joy is not as easy as it sounds. He thought that its successful implementation suggested nearing enlightenment. Which is a very big deal! As usual, though, Buddha isn't asking us to perfect this practice, but merely to try. In so doing, he promises we will feel an alleviation of jealousy.

Start with really encouraging yourself to feel the joy that your loved ones feel. Ignore distractions and invest in their joy. Then do the same with someone not as close to you – a random at work, for example. Next time there's an all-staff email telling you that Jenny from accounts has passed her exams and is now a fully qualified chartered accountant, remove that trigger finger from the delete button and take a moment to feel joy for her. Fire off a reply-all, congratulate her on what must have been a hard slog, and imagine how relieved she must be that all her studying is over. Really imagine it. It might even inspire you to stop by her desk on the way to the loo, to give her a heartfelt smile.

Okay, so far so good. Now, when next you hear of something wonderful that's happened for someone else and you feel jealousy creeping up on you, think through all the reasons why it's great news. Think about how proud their parents must be, about how much the extra money will change their lives, or about a time when they were disappointed by something and how wonderful it is that this thing happened instead. Let it give you faith that your day will come too if you stick with it. Remember how good it felt when Jenny from accounts so clearly couldn't believe you cared about her news and how stoked she was to see you actually took joy in it.

Making other people happy feels great. It feels even better when they don't expect it. Making other people happy by turning your own feelings from miserable jealousy into joy is a revelation. Try it for yourself.

Telling ourselves that someone has broken our hearts, leaving us angry, bitter, jealous and depressed, gives them a hell of a lot of power in our lives, doesn't it? When we say that, we're telling ourselves that our hearts and actions are out of our control, to be stolen and broken, used up and spat out at someone else's whim. In doing so, we relinquish responsibility for our own emotions. We characterise ourselves as helpless, faultless things. We are neither, luckily.

We are responsible for everything we do and say and feel, and that is truly wonderful news because it means that we must never suffer this badly ever again! It is going to take some work though.

PRIDE

There is definitely pride attached to being in a relationship. Whether it's our first relationship or our thirty-first, we feel good about the fact we've snared someone. It reassures us that we're loveable and attractive. If you've recently split with someone, you might be keen to let *them* know you're still loveable and attractive.

I'm at an age now where some of my male friends are experiencing classic midlife crises, in which they want to see if they're still desirable to women other than their wives. While they roll their eyes and tease each other about it, they're still undeniably impressed when a mate pulls a younger woman. I'm reliably informed that there's a euphoric rush of pride that goes along with acquiring and showing off a younger girlfriend, but it tends to wear off within months, when the daily grind of life reasserts itself. Even beautiful young women have jobs and bills to pay. Beautiful young women tend to grow older, and yearn at some point for commitment and family – which just so happens to be the situation their older lovers are fleeing from. Impermanence strikes again!

Just as our previous partners grew and changed, we must expect our next partners to do the same. Carefree young people become overwhelmed middle-aged people. The pressures of children, mortgages, careers – they happen. Of course we can personally choose to reject these things and make different life choices, but we can't make that decision for others, and we can't rely on others to continue to want an alternative lifestyle, any more than we can expect them to keep their hair the same way for sixty years.

Don't think I'm unfairly targeting men. I also have female friends in the *Eat, Pray, Love* camp who've decided there must be more to life than the monotony of raising a family. The most notable example I've ever come across emerged in a suburban brothel in Melbourne in the late '90s, where I was pulling the night shift as a receptionist.

A new girl called Amanda blew in one day, fresh from New Zealand, with a fabulous personality to match her cute, perky look. Where most girls wandered around the place in lingerie, Amanda always worked in a short, tight pencil skirt, a tight blouse and high but understated patent leather heals. She called it her 'slutty secretary' look and swore it was the key to her success. She was certainly successful, and had a long list of regular clients who kept her busy and financially secure, but Amanda also genuinely loved her work. She enjoyed the company of the men and made no bones about the thrill she got out of their desire for her. She said many times that she loved the fact that they would pay to have sex with her.

As we got to know Amanda better, she started telling us a few bits and pieces about her life, including the fact that she had two small sons and a husband back home in New Zealand. It wasn't a common story, but we weren't a judgemental bunch, so we didn't ask any further questions or really think much of it – until the night her sister arrived at the front door of the brothel looking for her. The story that unfolded astounded me and I still think about it often.

It turned out that Amanda had spent most of her life obese. She'd been given the role of the fat girl in her family and in her community, but somehow found the resolve in her mid-twenties to change herself and her life. She lost about 80 kilograms, and gradually Amanda started to feel attractive for the first time in her life. She was amazed and intoxicated by the fact that she could gain the sexual attention of men. Her pride in this newfound superpower compelled her to keep testing it, and, unsurprisingly, her marriage suffered. Eventually and unexpectedly, she walked out of her family home one morning and just never came back.

Thus began a two-year search by her family, which led her sister to Australia and to our brothel door. I called Amanda later to let her know what had happened, and told her what her sister had told us. Through shocked, embarrassed tears she confessed it was true. She also told me that the reason she loved being a prostitute so much was that no-one had ever desired her before, but now they desired her so much they paid to be with her. To her mind, that was wonderfully validating and it proved she was a different person to the fat girl her family wanted her to be. It was something of which she was immensely proud.

Buddha believed that Pride was an obstacle to compassion. I never knew Amanda's husband, or the ins and out of their relationship, but she spoke highly of him, and regretfully about the way it all ended. I do know that leaving her boys the way she did brought her a lot of pain and shame, and was no doubt confusing and frightening for them too. Amanda had every right to move to Australia and become a sex worker, but because of the heady, intoxicating pride, she acted hastily, lost contact with her sons, upturned the lives of everyone she loved and made it very difficult for herself when she wanted to go back, a couple of weeks after her sister's visit. Amanda grasped for the feelings of pride, acceptance, attractiveness and sophistication sex work gave her, and because of that she walked away from her family in a very uncompassionate way. These were all observations she made herself, during our phone call that night.

No-one suffered more for Amanda's pride than she did, although she expressed tremendous guilt when it came to her husband. She'd really rubbed her pride in his face, and let him know that she could now get 'better' men than him interested in her.

An ex's pride can be excruciatingly painful. When they're parading around with a new love, or bragging about their Tinder adventures, making it clear they're super stoked they moved on from you, it's easy to let your self-esteem shrink accordingly.

Adrian and I have done none of that stuff (yet), but just seeing him really happy and relaxed dents my pride some-times, I must admit. I made a joke of it to my dad once, and it's become a running thing between us. 'Jeez, he's really kicking goals without you driving him mad,' Dad will say with a laugh. Believe it or not, I actually do find it funny and it takes the sting out of it quite a bit.

I know Adrian feels it too sometimes, but we both try to keep the focus on Impermanence. Adrian would not call himself Buddhist, but he's really good at it, and he constantly reminds and reassures me that we had both changed, which is completely normal, and while we'd had a great marriage for a long time, we were now better as friends. Accepting Impermanence in a relationship has many benefits, but pride can keep us from admitting our own changes to ourselves.

I have a friend who didn't want children when she met her partner and now she does. The problem is they agreed in those early days that it was a core value of their relationship. They were not going to breed. As far as he knew, it was still the case. They'd spent their early years sniffing at crying babies on planes, cringing at messy families in cafes and rolling their eyes at each other whenever a couple they knew proudly announced and imminent arrival. To be frank, they were pretty condescending towards people who wanted kids.

Well, they're both impermanent of course, both still arising, and even the closest of couples will arise in different ways, influenced by environmental, karmic and yes, even hormonal factors. Impermanence will always keep things interesting, that's for sure. Let's face it: impermanence can often lead to difficult challenges like that one, and pride only makes it more difficult to admit to and accept changes in attitudes.

My friend didn't tell her partner her feelings had changed. She was too proud to admit that she had become one of those people they'd made fun of together for years. Instead, she hoped her partner would reach the same change of heart independently. As she waited and waited, seething inside, she told herself that immaturity was the problem – *his* problem. She reasoned that she had grown to a level of maturity where she understood that having children was the right thing to do. He kept voicing his relief at not having kids, as he'd always done, but instead of agreeing with him, my friend harboured resentment and started calling him a pathetic baby man at the slightest provocation. She lost all compassion for him, and he knew she had but didn't know why.

She finally blurted it out one day: 'You won't give me a child and it's too late for me to find someone else!'

He was blindsided, and this very important question had to be negotiated from an intensely emotional and uncompassionate starting point.

I wish I could tell you the story has a happy ending for one of them at least, but so far it's an ongoing conversation.

And as any woman who's found herself wanting a child in her late thirties will know, it is a very stressful situation.

When our attitudes evolve, we can be tempted to change partners and find someone who agrees with us about things as we see today. But we have to expect that at some stage in the future we'll disagree with them about something important too. Changing partners is not necessarily a recipe for happiness: it depends on why we we're unhappy. Sometimes pride prevents us from accepting that it's our fighting against reality that's making us unhappy. We can't turn back time, even by shacking up with someone who reminds us of our younger selves. I should say, *especially* by shacking up with someone else, because in my experience spending time with much younger people just tends to highlight the ways in which we're no longer young! Unfortunately, pride can convince us to leave relationships when what we really want to do is leave ourselves.

The problematic behaviours and consequences that come from the disturbing emotion of pride can be wide-ranging. I've seen some rather embarrassing attempts to reclaim one's youth that have ended in physical injury. Achilles tendons seem to be particularly susceptible to snapping under the pressure of 45-year-old bodies dancing, jumping on trampolines or kicking footies with 25-year-olds.

Prideful delusions can also create distance in relationships with people who are more grounded in reality. It can make it hard to believe that our partner is really leaving us. It can keep us waiting around for an ex's return rather than getting on with our lives, and make it difficult for friends and family members to communicate with us. Children can feel like they have to lie about one parent to the other, and that's obviously a terrible and damaging outcome for them and their arising. In other words, it's the kind of situation that can have a debilitating effect on their relationships in adulthood.

The antidote to pride is easy, just think about all the things you've said and done that you aren't proud of. Be sure to apply wisdom to know when to stop beating yourself up! There's no point in swinging from pride straight to self-hatred. Just remind yourself that you're not all that, and you'll be fine. Also, try subjugating yourself every once in a while, by which I mean allowing others to go first through a door, or in a line. Resist the urge to correct someone, even when you know they're wrong and it's a great opportunity for you to prove how clever you are. Assure the young person at the fast-food counter that you're not in a hurry. These are all good exercises in humility, the opposite of pride.

KEY POINTS

- Disturbing emotions are not hard to identify. They are things like anger, greed, jealousy, hate, pride, delusion and bitterness.

- Disturbing emotions are defensive emotions that erupt out of us when we are challenged. They lead to bad behaviour, which in turn leads to more problems. They are usually masking much deeper hurts or instincts.

- Peace is more beneficial than happiness. It lasts longer and is helpful to more people.

- Our peacefulness benefits the world, and also *our* world, as in our relationships.

- We must discipline ourselves and take responsibility for our emotions. Our partners are not responsible for making us happy or unhappy.

- Anger makes us vulnerable. *Don't engage* with people when they try to spark your anger. Walk away.

- Holding on to anger is like drinking poison and expecting the other person to die. Use those techniques such as taking deep breaths or counting to ten. These are about giving yourself a chance to collect your thoughts and react mindfully, rather than instinctively (which is often negative and over the top).

- When you feel your anger rising, walk away (Renee).

- The antidote to anger is patience. Cultivate patience by setting your intention every morning: 'Today I will be more patient.'

- When you hate someone, you are their prisoner. Try not to hate your ex, okay?

- Jealousy is an inevitable part of breaking up and moving on. But your ex-partner's post-break-up success does not mean your failure. Their new life is irrelevant to you.

- Work on unselfish joy – feel happiness for others.

- Pride is an obstacle to compassion. It prevents us from treating ourselves and others with kindness. Pride can lead us to act hastily, to enter into inappropriate and fake relationships.

- Changing partners won't make you happy if what you really want to change is yourself.

SELF-REFLECTION

- When we are angry around others, we want them to be scared of us. Are you wielding your anger as a weapon in relationships?

- Use mindfulness to investigate how much underlying anger and resentment there is in your life and your relationships. What are you *really* angry about?

- Try calling out your jealousy. Admit you're jealous and see how it feels.

- Are you paying too much attention to what other people are doing? Delete those social media connections!

6

Change

Odds are, if you're reading this book you are actively seeking change, although you might not have consciously realised it. Maybe the idea even terrifies you. But here you are, paying good money for tips on getting through a break-up, which suggests to me that you want to change the way you've been doing it.

Whether you initiated the break-up or were unceremoniously dumped, the place you find yourself in now is not good and you want to change it, right? Well, in order for you to feel differently in the world, eventually you have to change the way you react to it.

If you want to change your reactions, it has to come from within, from the way you treat and speak to yourself. It has to be a quiet, peaceful and personal revolution. You have to do it alone. You have to embrace change.

The kinds of changes that break-ups bring about can seem like a long shopping list of losses. On a very practical level, we can lose our homes, our pets, our friends, our income and even our children. We can feel as though everything we've worked for has been taken from us in the cruellest of circumstances, by someone we once loved and trusted.

If that's how you're feeling, I want to give you permission right here and now to *feel* it. Feel it all the way from the soles of your feet to the end of every frazzled strand of hair on your head. Scream it out or cry about it if that's what you need to do. Don't let those feelings nibble away at you slowly. Challenge them. Face them. Chase them down the rabbit hole and see for sure where they lead. You could spend the rest of your life worrying about what's at the bottom of that hole, afraid to move in any direction in case you fall in. Don't worry about it. Hurl yourself down there headfirst. You'll be amazed how deep and mysterious it *isn't*!

If you've already done that, and gone all the way with those feelings, you'll know they lead nowhere profound or helpful. All there is down there is exhaustion, disbelief and sadness, and there's only so long we can stay in that dark place. There's only so many times we can say 'I can't believe this is happening to me' before we get bored with it.

It's happening. So what are you going to do about it?

Eventually we all find ourselves standing up and moving towards the light. This is a critical moment. We can decide to hibernate some more, or we can choose to break free, seek out ideas, find inspiration and creatively solve our problems. We can change our lives for the better.

I lost my home in our break-up. All my adult life I'd dreamt of having a 'forever home' that my children would grow up in and come back to visit with their own families. I really thought I'd found it when we bought a quirky renovator's dream in a peaceful beachside suburb.

I spent the next four years slowly rejuvenating it, really unleashing my creativity because I had no intentions of ever selling it so I didn't care what anyone else thought of my design ideas. We ended up with a big timber fort for the kids, the Taj Mahal of chook pens, a lovely backyard full of greenery and birds that could be seen from every room in the house, lots of indoor plants, a mural in the bathroom, a kitchen backsplash made of huge black stones from India, a walk-in linen cupboard, floor-to-ceiling bookshelves in the living room, just like on *The Cosby Show*, and an industrial fridge. It was magnificent. My dream come true.

Then we decided to divorce. It was only eight weeks after I'd had the high pine ceilings painted white – a job I'd saved for and fantasised about since the day we moved in.

'My beautiful ceiling,' I moaned to my mother when I told her the news.

'What a shame,' she sighed down the phone.

We put the house on the market so that we could divide the spoils and get on with our independent lives, and it was bought by a developer who'd smash it to smithereens as soon as the permits came through to replace it with townhouses. My backsplash would be gone forever.

Oh man, it still takes a lot of emotional discipline to deal with the pain that comes up when I think about that house!

Anyway, the kids and I found another place. It's not near the beach or walking distance from their school like our old place, but it's strong and secure, and as luck would have it has the best chook house I've ever seen in my life, so that's something.

'You'll make it beautiful, Mum,' my daughter said to me when I took them for their first look at the big, empty, brown brick tank of a house.

I'll certainly do my best, I thought, and I remembered how much fun it was putting the last house together. All the Google-Image-searching, window-shopping and bargain-hunting. All the hours on Pinterest and Gumtree ... The more I thought about it, the more excited I got about the possibilities.

My turnaround wasn't just about having an excuse to shop and search late into the night for online home wares, although that *is* my favourite pastime. My change of outlook was mainly due to the reminder of Impermanence, and nothing reminds you of Impermanence like selling the house you thought you'd live in until you died. It was hard to accept that that house was not going to be my permanent home, but thinking about it reminded me that nothing lasts forever, nothing good and nothing bad, and the longer I live, the more comfort I draw from that fact. For me personally, the knowledge that bad times pass is worth knowing that good times are fleeting as well.

Until this point we've talked about Impermanence and Dependent Arising as fairly subtle forces, and in a lot of ways we do evolve slowly most of the time. Like climbing vines, our growth is imperceptible to the naked eye. Every now and then you see an old photo or try to fix a fence and realise that weedy little sapling has grown into a mighty vine.

People usually grow and change that way too. There are sometimes moments in life that change us suddenly, but for the most part, it happens slowly, so that we can turn around one day and realise we don't like the music or the clothes or the weather we used to. Yes, I did say weather. I've spent most of my life trying to avoid the sun and telling anyone who'd listen that I hate the heat. Over the last couple of years, though, I've become one of those people who's fixated with Bali. Now I spend months drooling over Bali pictures on Facebook and Instagram, and saving for my annual two weeks among the motorbikes and Bintang singlets of Sanur, Seminyak and Jimbaran Bay. My family can't believe it, but there you are. It's just one of the ways in which I am not the person I used to be.

I'm also more relaxed, less prone to yelling and anger, more comfortable with my physical appearance and I can run on a treadmill for twenty minutes without stopping. I've changed. Gradually, but definitely, I've become a different person – as has Adrian, and we are no longer a compatible romantic couple.

Our break-up has been brought about by change, and the break-up itself has changed us, as yours will you. The trick here is to accept it's inevitable and do your best to steer it in a positive direction. You can't fight change, or cower from it hoping it just somehow works out okay. You have to make the effort to influence your change. You have to make change your bitch!

Break-ups are the kind of life events that force you to think about how you deal with change, whether you're ready or not. By their very nature, break-ups leave you all alone with big decisions.

We often feel pressure from others to hurry up and change during a break-up. Everyone you know wants to talk about it, and they all want to know your 'plan'.

'What are you going to do about getting the kids to school?' is the question I was asked by every single person I knew when I told them about our break-up. They all knew I had to be at work by 5.30 a.m., and they all wanted to know what I was going to do about that.

The answer was that my lifestyle was going to have to change in some way. Was I going to get an au pair? Was I going to get a live-in nanny? Was I going to move in with my parents?

I know that tossing up between a nanny and an au pair sounds like a problem J-Lo might have – i.e. pretty luxurious – but as expensive as these options are, it felt like it was either that or quit my job. I was going to be broke either way, but I *really* didn't want to live with my parents!

I've had friends who've sworn by their international au pairs, until they had to sack one – then it wasn't so much cross-cultural fun. One friend sacked a mopey German because she cried all the time, and another gave a horny Pole the heave-ho when she was caught inviting men around when they were out. There is no easy answer when it comes to child care, particularly for a single parent.

I didn't know what I was going to do about the kids in the mornings, but I knew I'd figure something out. As it turned out, Adrian and I figured out a plan between us, and my sister chipped in to help, so it's sorted for now, but no doubt it'll change at some point. I'm not going to worry about what I'll do then though. I'll just stick with the here and now, which is challenging enough.

It's very difficult, when people are demanding to know your plans, to admit you're lost and don't have any answers, so often you do what a lot of humans do in these situations – you lie! You tell them what you're going to do about it all – a list of bullet points that changes every day and with everyone you speak to depending on what you think they'll approve of – you say whatever will make them stop asking.

I'm all for lying to other people to get them off your back, believe me, but you have to be honest with yourself. As tempting as it is, don't believe your own bullshit; don't comfort yourself with fantasies. You will need a good plan at some point, but it has to start with pulling yourself together and coming to terms with the changes.

I know that even thinking about change is enough to get some people's hearts racing. They'll tell you very clearly that they don't like change. They'll probably say it sternly while looking directly into your eyes. They might even press the stiffened palms and splayed fingers of their hands towards you as if to hold the threat of your changeable self at bay. Yep, some people really hate change. My ex-husband Adrian is one of them. Honestly, I think one of the things that prevented him from leaving our relationship was his crippling fear of change.

Adrian's the type of person who'd turn to me two years after we'd moved house and tell me he finally feels like he's settled in. Unfortunately, that's usually about the time I'm getting a bit bored and thinking about exploring another suburb and another house. Incompatible much?

Adrian and I somehow became a pretty great team despite all of our conflicting desires, and I guess we both developed a bit of a 'better the devil you know' attitude about relationships. As much as our fundamental differences drove us crazy and meant that at least one of us was feeling pretty frustrated most of the time, we managed to run a home, a family and a life together, and I think we probably worried how we'd manage to do that apart. We worried about how our lifestyles would change.

Even the most easygoing person can hang onto a relationship a bit longer than they should because they're daunted by the changes a break-up will bring about.

Break-ups slap us in the face with Impermanence and they keep slapping us with every outdated opinion, view, perception and label we were still applying to the relationship. The break-up taunts us with the evidence that the relationship we thought we had didn't actually exist. At best, it may have belonged to two people who existed in the past but don't exist anymore, because you are no longer them. So much so, the break-up tells us, that upon reflection, it's been determined by at least one party that you are no longer two compatible people who enjoy being together in a romantic relationship at all. You are no longer *in love*.

It might not have been described quite that way in the note they left on the fridge, but that's the egg and beans of it.

It's probably the case that the person who was first honest with themselves about it was the one who brought about the break-up, one way or another. It's also likely that the other person wasn't ready for that honesty: in fact, they might have preferred to live out their lives ignoring the niggling feeling that something wasn't right and avoiding the terrifying soul-searching that comes with undeniable, monumental change. Ironically, in our case, it was fear-phobe Adrian who realised first, and brave Buddhist Meshel who clung so hard to delusion.

I actually think we're all aware of Dependent Arising and Impermanence on a profoundly deep level. We all know that we are being shaped by our environment every minute of every day. We can get used to a certain life, with a particular person, in a particular house, and we can convince ourselves we're not really changing at all, or if we are it's very slow and we're pretty sure we know what it's going to look like anyway. Leaping into an unknown life is threatening because we don't know who it's going to turn us into.

As we discussed earlier, there was a chance that if I stayed with Adrian I'd gradually grow into one of the old ladies at the hairdressers, still living in the same house with the same man, getting the same haircut every six weeks. By leaving that life, I've had to face up to an unknown future and an unknown future self. What if I evolve into a lonely old woman who lies dead in her house for years undiscovered, with her TV still flashing because her direct debits are paying her bills like a dream, but no-one in the world cares to visit, let alone live their life with her?

Yeesh. Change can really freak you out if you let it. It can make you feel like you don't know anything anymore. I've certainly felt that way during the breaking up process.

Now, what we *should* do in this situation is take it as a wake-up call and meditate on Emptiness. We should reapproach life with a clear, open mind and rethink everything we thought we knew. We should be all about new strategies, new ways of communicating, and working on seeing both ourselves and others as new people and forgetting everything we thought we knew. We should drill down into our disturbing emotions while cultivating compassion for both ourselves and our exes.

We should do all of that while eating a low-fat, high-fibre diet. We should drink eight glasses of water a day, stretch after exercising, catch up on our taxes and call our mothers more often. We should read more, text less and flip our mattress every three months.

If only we always did what we should, huh?

If you're not quite ready to apply yourself to a full-blown spiritual awakening, that's okay. There are other ways of feeling better about the big changes break-ups bring. Here are a few.

CREATE A COMFORTABLE LIVING ARRANGEMENT FOR YOURSELF

Break-ups can lead to some diabolical living situations. Are you on a couch at your mate's? Are you back at Mum's? Are you still living with or near your ex? Make it your mission to get out of there. Move to a cheaper, less impressive suburb and get a flatmate if you have to: it'll be worth it. When you give yourself back the feeling of having a home, you'll be more able to tackle the big stuff. Plus you won't have to talk to your mum about your break-up. Oh God, anything but that.

GET A HAIRCUT

I'm a big believer in the break-up haircut. I'm growing out a mohawk as we speak, which is a nightmare, but God, it was so worth it. I got the haircut I'd wanted since I was fourteen and it was brilliant. Hair grows back, which makes it the perfect metaphor for Impermanence. The place between mohawk and anything else is just a kind of weird, inverted, side mullet, but I've recently discovered hair extensions and they're making my head look quite normal. It just goes to show there's always something they can do if you go for broke with your hair and it's a disaster. Like the old joke says: 'What's the difference between a bad haircut and a good haircut? About two weeks.'

GROOMING

Get on top of maintenance generally. Get in the shower and get stuck in to whatever you've been neglecting.

WATCH YOUR DRUNK BEHAVIOUR

Don't get drunk alone or with anyone who'll let you drunk dial, drunk text, drunk tweet, drunk Facebook, drunk Instagram or, heaven forbid, drunk visit. Give a friend the authority to confiscate your phone at any time. In all seriousness, don't set yourself up to fail, don't create a perfect storm of regret for yourself. Take responsibility, be a grown up, and create a space in which you can succeed. If that means going for movies and ice-cream with your mum instead of Jaegar bombs and body shots with the girls from work, then so be it.

CRY IT OUT

Cry it out – either with friends or alone, whatever works for you, but not in the work toilets. They'll call you 'crying Jenny from accounts' forever. If you indulge in a big, ugly cry in an appropriate time and place, it's less likely to explode from your face when you don't want it to.

TELL YOUR STORY

Tell the entire story of your relationship and break-up from your perspective, out loud, to yourself (not to anyone else – I repeat: to yourself) and don't spare the outrage. Really ramp it up as though Oprah herself is gasping at the injustice of it all. It honestly helps and doesn't bore anyone else and you can do it as many times as you need to.

GIVE YOURSELF TIME

If you push yourself into a cheap fling with a young spunk to prove your indomitability to the world too early, it can back-fire. You may well end up on a public toilet floor vomiting expensive hipster hamburgers without your phone because your bestie confiscated it before making off with the young spunk you put dibs on while shouting shots for the whole bar. Or so I've heard.

I remember when I was pregnant, a friend who'd not long ago had her first baby told me to accept that the first couple of months were going to be a write-off. She told me that if I managed to have a shower every day I'd be doing well, and that wearing nothing but track pants was a very sensible option. Under no circumstances she said, was I to attempt to pull myself together and present a perfect picture of confident motherhood to the world while breastfeeding twins eight times a day and recovering from a caesarean.

I took her advice and I was very happy I did. It came back to me recently when thinking about my break-up. I realised that the break-up had been similarly massive in terms of life upheaval, and that I had to give myself time to be able to stand up straight again, like I did after my babies were born. My job isn't to make other people comfortable with my break-up, or to give everyone the impression that I'm a superwoman who just brushed it off and powered on.

Buddha insisted upon generosity and kindness as means of maintaining humility and of liberating oneself from feelings of separateness from others. We spoke earlier about generosity as a way of putting our difficulties into perspective so as not to become self-absorbed. Well, now we see that there are times when we need to be kind to ourselves, too, to remind ourselves that we're still part of the world and as worthy of compassion as anyone.

Also, we are frankly lucky to have this precious human life, with which to study the Dharma and be of service to others, so it's incumbent upon us to care for ourselves so that we may live long, useful lives. Do what you have to do to rebuild your strength and get back into the world.

If you're not ready yet, hopefully at some point you'll move into the more demanding Buddhist techniques. Take your time, they're not going anywhere, but neither are the challenges in your life, which will no doubt come knocking if you try to ignore them for too long.

When Adrian and I went public with our split, I found change in the most unexpected of places. Suddenly the fun chats with my female friends about our lives and families seemed loaded. I felt like they stopped themselves in the middle of funny stories about their husbands like they felt sorry for me or were worried I only had heartbreaking stories to share in return. Maybe they just felt guilty about their playful complaints – at least their marriage was still intact. I felt awkward too. I didn't have a husband anymore, but what on earth had I done with him? Was he behind the couch cushions? Was he in the bottom of the tumble dryer with the odd socks? He'd just vanished. I mean, I knew where Adrian was physically, but where had the *concept* of him gone, the other half of me? One day I could say, 'My husband ...', and the next day, I couldn't. Could I still share funny stories of his ineptitude or would it seem bitter now?

What was I going to call him in these strange new circumstances? My ex-husband? Oh God, that seemed very final and very foreign. Was I really a person with an ex-husband? Was that really my new identity, with all the baggage of settlements and snide remarks and kids-access-weekend-drop-offs that go with it?

I started to realise there were a lot of things I hadn't thought about pre-break-up, things I couldn't think about because I didn't know about them. I had known my life would change, but I didn't know in how many ways. It felt at first as though it had been picked up by a tornado and I just had to wait to see where and how everything landed. Later I realised I had to be more proactive than that. I had to treat it like a three-ring circus featuring my ex-husband, his family, my family, our children, their teachers, our friends, my workmates, our lawyers, our mediators, financial advisers and nosy neighbours, with me as the ringmaster juggling them all.

My parents, who'd always loved Adrian, became wary, and he of them. His family begged me not to keep the kids from them. As if I would! Our children played us off against each other and fibbed about things we'd said and not said, and their teachers sent two sets of notes home urging us to update our personal info ASAP in case one of us was suddenly not to be contacted in an emergency or allowed on the school grounds. Our friends advised us individually not to trust each other over money, as did our lawyers and financial advisers, who between them told us not to talk to each other about anything at all! My workmates signed me up to Tinder. Talk about changes!

As ringmaster, I gave myself permission to handle things my way, in accordance with what felt right to me. I took advice, but I applied my own moral compass.

I remember asking my dad to cultivate compassion for Adrian after a particularly dramatic and unpleasant bust-up, and I don't think he knew whether to laugh or cry. He definitely thought it was bizarre and told me so, but I had to be gentle with him too, and tell him that this was how I needed to handle it, for my own peace. That particular event could easily have changed the entire course of our break-up, as we both ended up with lawyers champing at the bit to turn it into

World War III. We managed to bring it back under control though, by ignoring everyone else and talking to each other.

The one thing we both know for sure is that Impermanence is here to stay, baby. Our lives will change many times over, and the day we give up on working at it together is the day we each lose a part of our kids.

There is, of course, an upside to change/Impermanence – no matter how much pain and fear you're feeling now, it won't last forever because nothing, not even your poor broken old heart stays the same forever. Your feelings of betrayal won't last, your shock and anger will pass, and even your anxiety will wear itself out at some stage. Thich Nhat Hanh put this positive spin on it: 'Thanks to impermanence, everything is possible.'

The bad news is that none of us has a road map for our post-break-up lives, but the good news is that it's just because that map hasn't been drawn yet. We are drawing it with every step we take away from that relationship. We have an opportunity to redefine ourselves and move towards the person we want to be and the life we want to live. That may well start today with a haircut, or even just with a shower, but remember every day is a page in the story of your post-break-up life.

There's no doubt that a break-up will change a lot of aspects of your life, but we have to get on top of the 'future living' anxiety that comes from trying to foresee and strategise challenges that haven't happened yet. Some of the things we're most worried about will never happen; hopefully my unnoticed death is one of them! Some difficulties we never imagined will pop up and it will take everything we have to cope with them. That's life, and life after a break-up is no different really, even if it feels like a parallel dimension for a while.

Shortly we'll talk about the biggest change that's likely to come with a break-up – aloneness, the very thing many of us fear most. We've all fought too long for relationships just to avoid aloneness, haven't we?. Learning to live without fear of aloneness will change everything. It will help you see that change is inevitable, that it's about growth and that you can take control of it and ensure you're growing in a positive direction.

We can commune and support each other, we can meditate together and share ideas, but ultimately we need to be able to sit alone with ourselves, remind ourselves constantly of what we're trying to achieve and monitor our own progress. There's no-one else inside your head when your ex-partner starts pushing your buttons, or when your fear wants to push disturbing emotions to the fore. It's up to you to call 'time out' on yourself, to be honest with yourself about your instinctive reaction and to decide what you're going to do about it. You need to ask: 'Am I going to use this as an opportunity for change?'

That's another good one to use when you're setting your intention for the day: 'Today I will use every opportunity to change myself for the better.' If you remember it just once in a day, you're on your way.

When you're ready, you can focus on the exciting changes you can make. If your relationship was one of sadness and frustration for a long time, you now have a chance to create a life without those things. You can live in peace. You can choose how to spend your money without anyone else's input, you can choose everything from linen to pizza toppings without having to ask anyone else's opinion. Move the furniture, go where you want for Christmas, never fight for the blankets ever again! Figure out what really makes you happy as the person you are now, and perhaps down the road a bit you'll be part of a better kind of relationship.

KEY POINTS

- You want change. That's why you are reading this book.

- A break-up brings change. You determine whether it will change your life for the worse or for the better.

- We must get on top of the 'future living' anxiety that makes us fear change. Stay in the moment and don't look too far ahead. Don't imagine how your post-break-up life is going to play out.

- You are not the same individual who walked into the relationship. You've changed. Start seeing yourself as you really are now. Start taking responsibility for changing into the person you want to be.

- We are drawing the roadmap for our post-break-up lives right now.

- Impermanence is the reality of existence. Nothing stays the same. The pain and chaos of break-ups passes too, if you let it.

- Give yourself time for the dust to settle. Don't expect too much from yourself immediately after a break-up, but keep trying.

- Forgive yourself when disturbing emotions get out of control.

- When you're ready, focus on the exciting changes you can now make.

- Make the change to positivity and peace.

- Be wary of grand gestures of change and control, maybe think twice before doing something massive to prove you're getting on with life – real personal growth and change is where it's at.

SELF-REFLECTION

- In a challenging situation, ask yourself: 'Am I going to use this as an opportunity to change?'

7

Aloneness versus Loneliness

ALONENESS

The obvious and most immediate change that comes with a break-up is aloneness. As we discussed earlier, being in a relationship means belonging to something, even if that something is sad and dysfunctional. The shared history and companionship of a relationship can't be replicated with anyone else, and it leaves a big hole in your life when it disappears.

As a recently divorced friend of mine put it, 'No-one else gives a shit if your kid finally makes it to the top of the monkey bars. Now his mum's not here to tell that stuff to, I miss it. It seems a bit needy and sad to ring her and tell her. I've lost that day-to-day parenting partner and I feel very alone.'

Does my friend feel *alone* or *lonely* in those moments? There's a difference. And aloneness and loneliness call for different responses. The first thing we have to do, as always, is be honest with ourselves about what we're really feeling.

Loneliness, like jealousy, is an emotion we often feel embarrassed about. Loneliness has a certain vibe of blame attached, like it's the lonely person's fault. There's an expectation that you should be able to fix loneliness by going out more or making more of an effort. Maybe you could even fix it by being a more appealing person. All of that is unreasonable and unrealistic, as we'll see later in this chapter, but for now, let's focus on why we might feel a little bit more dignified in saying we're *alone*, rather than lonely.

I'm not mad at you for mislabelling it, by the way. Break-ups are so undignified!

When we say we feel alone after a break-up, it's strongly implied that we've been *left* alone. It's got an involuntary ring to it. Dare I say, a ring of victimhood? 'I feel very alone,' is the kind of thing we say when we feel overwhelmed and under-supported. It's a cry for help. It's a way of saying, 'I feel so abandoned.'

In saying this, I don't mean to diminish in any way the fact that some people really are terribly abandoned in relationships and break-ups. The friend I mentioned above has been victimised by his ex-wife in many ways over many years. She is an A-grade narcissist of the highest order! She rampaged through his life for twenty years and then made the divorce a living nightmare. I wouldn't dream of asking him to accept or even forget about that behaviour for Buddha's sake, and neither would Buddha!

I do, however, ask him to shift his focus for *his own* sake, and ground his emotions in the reality of now. It took a lot of time and effort to get to a place where he could live with some peace, and I can see how much better off my friend is without her – even if sometimes he feels alone.

Having initiated my own separation, I can relate to the strange emotional space my friend is in. However, I only initiated it because I felt like my husband had left me already in every way apart from physically. It creates a really confusing bundle of emotions.

I went to see a local psychologist about two years before our first separation, ostensibly about work stress, but in the final minutes of the hour-long session I said to her, 'Oh, and I also want you to help me pluck up the courage to end my marriage.'

I flip-flopped a hundred times a day between wanting to break up and not wanting to break up, and often it had nothing to do with anything Adrian was saying or doing at the time. It was the push and pull of my head and my heart – or, more accurately, my wisdom and my fear.

No matter how right you know a break-up is for you, you can still end up feeling let down by your ex, abandoned and alone. It comes back to feeling disappointed in them for not being who we wanted them to be, which in turn comes back to our ignoring reality in favour of fantasies.

My friend doesn't feel alone because the rampaging narcissist is no longer bankrupting him or screaming abuse at him; he feels alone because he's accepted that's who she actually is. He doesn't have a fantasy to cuddle up to anymore. He's investing a lot of his newfound spare time and emotional energy into thinking about that, which means his ex-wife is still controlling him. In hating her, he remains her prisoner. It's only hurting him, not her. How's she doing? Well, she was jaunting around the Pacific Islands with a new partner last I heard.

Like many of us, my friend avoided facing the fact that his ex was not a person with whom he wanted to live for a very long time. He employed lots of techniques to avoid the truth over the years: denial, fantasy, self-blame, alcoholism and workaholism. But now, he's had to face reality. It hurts and it's lonely. Clearly, he has much about which to feel angry, hateful, bitter, vengeful, afraid, and so on, but what good does all that do him?

His ex-wife has left him alone with traumatised kids and few resources with which to start his life again, but he is also free of her. The greatest benefit of not being in a relationship is the amount of time and energy we can invest in ourselves. Every moment we spend cursing an ex for leaving us alone is a moment wasted on old rubbish.

Let's embrace aloneness, people! Let's see it for what it is: an opportunity to practise some mad Buddhist skills. As a consequence of a break-up, we have a chance to really influence our own arising. Those of us with children know that divorcing parents is the biggest and most influential events of their lives. We can encourage an enormous amount of positive arising in our kids during this time, by showing them how to embrace Impermanence, reality and aloneness. I'm not pretending it's easy. My son has lately been telling me he's 'too little to have parents living in different houses'. It's devastating to hear him say that and to see the fat tears run down his face, but I have to stay in reality and deal with what really is. I have to keep reinforcing the fact that he is very loved by both his parents but we need our own space to stay happy and peaceful (and not fight).

Whether or not we have kids, in separating with confidence and grace, we can be a beacon to others. This might sound overblown, but I know that I, for one, have been inspired by other people's post-divorce success. Adrian's parents are an excellent example. They divorced very bitterly when he was a teenager, but in the years that followed built a real friendship together so as to both be able to attend family events without tension.

Aloneness isn't in and of itself unpleasant. Think of the most irritating person you know. Would you rather be sitting alone, or sitting with them? The answer should be obvious, unless you have a deep-seated fear of being alone and would rather anyone's company to your own.

There's a name for such extreme cases: monophobia. At it's worst, a sufferer refuses even to use the toilet without someone else in the room. It's an extreme kind of agoraphobia in which a person's self-confidence is so low they don't believe they can cope or keep themselves safe without the help and supervision of another person – sometimes one person in particular. If you have a serious fear of being alone, you need a good therapist who can help you unlock the reasons behind that. It's too much to lay on a partner.

However, even in a normal relationship, we come to depend on the other person in certain ways. In most relationships there's a kind of informal agreement about the division of daily labour. It might be: 'I work longer hours, so you cook dinner.' Or: 'You clean the kitchen, so I put the bins out.' Couples have informal agreements about a million other things that don't even seem logical when they're spoken out loud, but we come to rely heavily on these agreements. Maybe one person always cleans the shower, while the other always drops Nanna home after Christmas lunch. One organises the direct debits, and the other cleans up the backyard dog poo. One stacks the dishwasher and the other gets up to the kids at night.

Hopefully it all kind of evens out and both parties are at least peripherally aware that the other is taking care of stuff, but I can tell you from experience that suddenly shifting to running the house alone can be quite a shock. About a month or so into our first separation, as the grass grew long and brown and stank to high heaven of dog poo, I started to wonder how – and in fact *if* – I would be able to keep myself and the kids alive without Adrian's supervision and help. It was very overwhelming at times.

The feeling I was calling aloneness when I was still married, was actually loneliness and low self-esteem. I was feeling pretty useless and stupid at not having been able to keep my marriage together. What I should have done was work on my self-image, and take advantage of the solitude with some introspection. Low self-esteem relies on self-criticism. There's plenty of criticism flying around before, during and after a break-up, so it's no wonder it can infiltrate our inner monologue too. Rather than let it scare you away from introspection, let it be the reason to embrace it. Aloneness will help you hear the negative self-talk that's bringing you down, and when you hear it you'll know it's over the top. Only then can you really challenge it and work on reminding yourself of your strengths.

I didn't follow my own advice when I was suffering from low self-esteem. What I actually did was renege on the separation and practically beg Adrian to move back in. Things were different the next time around, though. I was better prepared for the reality of being alone, my kids were older and less dependent and I was more centred and confident. This time I focused on the fact that running the house alone is different but no harder than running a house with someone I can't live with without fighting. Being alone is certainly more peaceful!

I'm at the stage now where I consciously enjoy doing alone all the things that used to be fraught with controversy and tension when I tried to do them with Adrian. Just choosing something to watch on TV after a long day was a painful experience that almost always ended up unsatisfactorily for me. Now, as I lie alone in my big bed and watch whatever the hell I please, I can't help but sigh with relief. I'm relieved when I pack the kids lunchboxes, when I buy new things and when I let our pet chook inside on hot days, because there are no arguments anymore. Being alone is so wonderful!

But aloneness is not just about getting our own way: it gives us an opportunity to think. Thinking about our lives without distractions is the only way we can evolve thoughtfully into the person we want to be. If we spend our lives avoiding being alone with ourselves, just reacting to the world, grasping for short-term coping mechanisms and relying on others to tell us who we are, we'll end up pretty crudely carved by life. You can sometimes see it in people's faces, can't you? I can see in the faces of friends who've spent their lives using drugs or alcohol to avoid themselves: the random etchings of a life of emotional chaos. It sends shudders down my spine just thinking about it, it's so sad.

What is it that these people are afraid of? What do they think will happen if they're alone with themselves? Are they really afraid of what might happen? The frustrating thing about anxiety attacks, which I used to suffer from, is that when you really get down to it, a lot of it is anxiety about the anxiety attack itself. I remember worrying myself sick about what might happen if my attack progressed, which ensured it did. Eventually I realised that what always happened was it blew itself out. I didn't end up screaming or writhing around on the floor in public, as I sometimes feared I would: I just ended up tired. When I understood that, I stopped having anxiety attacks.

You need to figure out exactly what it is about being alone that scares you. Do you think you'll cry? Well, that's fine. Someone said to me once: 'I'm scared if I start crying I'll never stop.' Of course she *would* have stopped, but it seemed like a pretty sincere expression of fear to me.

Are you afraid of feeling sad? Do you worry about just how sad you might actually be? Maybe you'll discover you're really, *really* sad. But I guess you're already as sad as you are, right? Actually facing it isn't going to make it worse.

What if you sat alone with yourself, discovered you were really, properly sad, then cried for ages? Then what would happen? The answer is nothing, except possibly a feeling of relief at having released your feelings. If you sat alone again tomorrow, you might be sad and cry then too, but it wouldn't be as bad. And the day after tomorrow, it would be better still. We humans are incredibly resilient creatures. We are built to overcome and keep moving, and tears and sadness are part of that mechanism. Let your mind and body do what they need to do to repair.

Buddhism requires self-reflection. It doesn't actually work without it. You can read all the books, buy all the statues and share all the motivational memes you want, but if you're not prepared to sit alone with yourself, you're not actually doing it.

As you progress, it'll become easier and more natural, but in the beginning it takes a lot of discipline, and ideally it'll involve meditation. If you really can't do it yet – that is, spend time with yourself either meditating or just thinking about life, love and the universe – then reading Buddhist books is a great way to train your mind for reflection. No doubt you'll read bits that stop you in your tracks and have you blinking at the ceiling in bed later. If you find that all your worries seem to come and sit on your chest at night time, preventing you from sleeping, create a specific time and place in your day for meditation or quiet reflection so you can deal with all of that before bedtime. You can use the same technique with crying: allow yourself a specific time and place for a good cry, and you will find this will stop it happening when you don't want it to.

Aloneness is crucial in break-up recovery in particular, because you have so much to think about and grow from. There's an old joke about the point of marriage: 'Of course you need a wife, otherwise who would ever tell you all the things that are wrong with you?' There's a ring of truth to that, actually. I'm not suggesting every accusation that's hurled at you during a break-up is insightful, but I'm sure you noticed some issues in your ex when you got to know them well, especially if you lived with them, so it's probably likely they may have noticed a few of yours.

By exploring which of these nuggets of insight might have some truth in them, you can also free yourself of the unreasonable insults that weren't true and that you don't need to carry around. Of course, it takes skill to sort out the petty stuff from the constructive criticism, and by all means reach out to friends and professionals for guidance, but don't do that *instead* of introspection. It can't be out-sourced, I'm afraid.

Aloneness will give you the opportunity to drill down into your disturbing emotions, your attachments and your self-destructive behaviours. It's like a puzzle that will come together before your eyes, with surprising results. You'll find you're holding on to all sorts of things from as far back as early childhood that are affecting your emotional reflexes today. By naming them and filing them properly in the past, you don't have to keep living them over and over again. You can look forward to better relationships as a consequence of this alone time.

Knowing how to be solitary is central to the art of loving. When we can be alone, we can be with others without using them as a means of escape.

BELL HOOKS

That reminds me: although your post-break-up instinct might be to surround yourself with people to prove you're loveable and to distract yourself from your real feelings and fear, at some point you're going to have to close the door and be alone with yourself. Friends and family need to get on with their lives eventually, as do neighbours, random hook-ups, checkout operators, hairdressers, bar tenders, pizza delivery drivers, call-centre operators and anyone else you might be relying on to listen to you and save you from being alone.

Rather than run out of company, why not take the initiative and go solo of your own free will? Here are some suggestions for dipping your toe into the aloneness pool that hopefully won't sound sad or scary.

- Go for a walk – either around your block or drive to somewhere more scenic. Leave the headphones at home unless you are going to listen to a guided walking meditation. Even moderate exercise releases endorphins that interact with receptors in your brain to actually reduce your perception of pain, both physical and emotional. It's virtually impossible to not feel better after a walk, so why wouldn't you? Why the hell don't *I*? I must get onto that.

- Maybe sit for a bit somewhere along the way, but not somewhere with lots of distractions. Cafes are hopeless for aloneness. If you don't pick up the paper or bury yourself in your phone, the wait staff will feel sorry for you and strike up a conversation. Why not grab a takeaway coffee and sit in the park instead.

- Is there a spot around your house that could work? I hate to say it, but it was the one benefit I could see of being a smoker. Whenever Adrian starts to wig out, he excuses himself and goes outside to sit on his smoking chair for a while. There's an unwritten rule forbidding anyone from following him out there, and we sometimes have to wait some time for him to re-join the conversation (or argument), but when he does he's generally got a much more considered position on the topic. But you don't have to smoke to go outside and sit for ten or fifteen minutes by yourself. It might be worth investing in a comfortable outdoor setting to lure you there.

- If outside's not your thing, set up a nice sitting spot for yourself inside, maybe with a comfy chair by a window. If you build it, you just might come.

- Have a bath, but don't take a radio, a book or anything else to distract yourself with. Just lie in the warm water and breathe.

- Switch the TV off when there's nothing interesting on instead of watching something boring just to avoid the silence. Lie back on the couch and look at the ceiling for a little while.

Just five minutes of this sort of quiet time a day is enough to have a profound impact on your life.

Creating a consistent practice of aloneness will help you find clarity about what you really want from relationships and what compromises you're prepared to make. Won't you be frustrated with yourself if, a year from now, you're repeating the mistakes of your last relationship with somebody else? Well, just don't! It's in your hands and in your aloneness. In order to avoid it, you must be very clear about what 'it' is.

Being alone might make you realise how often you apologise, run around after others or people-please. You might get a sense of the neediness you bring to relationships, or of the constant distraction-seeking that makes intimacy difficult. When you give yourself a break from your usual patterns, you might see how much pressure you put on yourself socially. You might find you're never really relaxed around others, or that you don't let your guard down easily. You might find you struggle to nominate a purpose to your life when you can't take care of other people. These can all be factors in unsuccessful relationships, but they can be hard to identify without opting out completely for a little while.

It won't only be your romantic relationships that benefit. My ex-husband complained about my prioritising work above all else. Through self-reflection I realised he was right. I was no longer in a place in my career where I had to say yes to every opportunity or gratefully drop everything at a moment's notice to pick up some extra work. But I hadn't moved on from the fear of that time in my life; the regrettable behaviour that resulted from that disturbing emotion was neglect of my family. As a result of his criticism and my taking time alone to really ponder it, I work much less now and spend more time with my children, which is obviously great for my relationship with them.

Learning to spend time alone confidently and happily will only strengthen your position in future relationships. Once you take the fear of being alone out of the equation, you're much more likely to nip bad relationships in the bud and save yourself a lot of time and hassle. You won't find yourself sitting frozen beside a lake on a Saturday afternoon watching grown men race model boats, thinking, 'What the hell am I doing here? Oh that's right, this is where *he* is and I don't want to be alone.'

No, you don't need to do that. You can stay home in your Snuggie working on your emotional and spiritual evolution – or colouring for mindfulness, if that's your thing – to your heart's content. Being okay with being alone means never having to feign interest in someone else's hobby, or having to hide your own, ever again. Surely it's worth it!

LONELINESS

We've now seen how aloneness can be positive. But loneliness is something else altogether. Adrian and I visited a (different) psychologist as part of our divorce mediation process. We only saw her on one day, first together and then individually, but boy, did she have our number! By the time she and I met alone she was all over our issues. But there was one question in particular she wanted to ask me: 'Are you worried about being lonely?'

It was disarming, because no-one ever asks that question directly, but I answered without hesitation: 'I've been lonely for years.'

Other people expect us to feel lonely after a break-up. I've had more than one sympathetic friend comment on how lonely I must feel alone in bed at night. But as I've explained, that feeling of loneliness was more prevalent before the break-up than after it, and now being alone in bed is one of my favourite situations in which to be!

What I'm getting at is: don't let others convince you you're lonely, because with the best intentions in the world, they will try to. They'll organise outings, they'll phone and text, they might even try to rush you into dating. Through introspection (if they leave you alone long enough to perform any), you'll figure out your true feelings and needs. I was quite surprised to discover that post-break-up I didn't feel much loneliness at all, certainly not on a day-to-day basis. I felt much lonelier when Adrian and I were still supposedly in a relationship yet he was clearly avoiding me.

I've discovered that for me, loneliness is closely associated with future thinking. It pops up when I think about something I might want to do in the future that's traditionally an activity for couples. For example, the other night some workmates were discussing restaurants. They'd both recently celebrated milestone birthdays by treating themselves and their partners to an expensive meal at a world-class restaurant. Their conversation piqued my interest and I considered, for a brief moment, looking into going to one of these places. Then it hit me like a punch in the gut: was I going to go alone?

In that moment of realisation that I don't have anyone in my life with which to share such an experience, I felt very lonely. But I hadn't felt lonely until I started projecting into the future, which as we know is pointless because none of us knows what the future will bring. There's every chance I will re-partner and visit nice restaurants on big birthdays, and there's every chance I won't, but letting those future possibilities affect my mood in this moment is pretty silly.

What I do know for sure is that Adrian and I tried many 'date nights' in nice restaurants and more often than not we barely spoke and I ended up feeling very lonely in the moment.

Loneliness is quite abstract and conceptual. Mother Theresa said, 'Loneliness and the feeling of being unwanted is the most terrible poverty.' We can feel loneliness when we are surrounded by people, and we can also be devoid of loneliness when alone, so it's obviously more complicated than simply not having company.

Loneliness is the poverty of self. Solitude is the richness of self.

MAY SARTON

As we've discussed, learning to be confidently alone is a very powerful skill. It allows us time to process and grow, but it also protects us from poor company. When you're unafraid of being alone, you find yourself in the company of jerks much less often. Now that is richness of self!

We can be happily alone with ourselves when we know we're connected to all beings. If we forget that, to the extent that we don't feel connected to the people right there beside us, that's loneliness.

As with everything else, fixing the loneliness problem takes effort. It's not going to just happen, and no-one else can fix it for you. It requires an understanding of Emptiness – removing the labels we've placed on people and things. 'This house is lonely now' is an example of something we might've said before remembering that the house itself is just a house. It's up to us how we see the house, and we can just as easily label the house 'peaceful', 'gentle', 'spacious' or 'harmonious'.

The first time Adrian and I separated, I did one of the most hysterical, ridiculous things I've ever done: I painted the entire interior of my house bright green, orange and yellow. The yellow in particular was so bright it literally made my eyes blurry to look at it. I painted at night, while the kids were in bed, slopping paint all over the uncovered floors and windows. My twins were only three at the time, so god knows what they thought when they wandered out in the mornings to find another couple of walls blaring at them and their mother asleep on the couch with paint spattered in her hair. I was not aware at that time that I was connected to all things – I was barely aware I was connected to my own babies. I was terrified of introspection, obsessed with future thinking, grasping for a quick fix – and I thought I had to change the house to prevent me from missing Adrian's presence in it. I was so terrified of loneliness, I never even stopped to check to see if I was feeling any.

Even if you have checked, checked and checked again and you're screaming at me now 'I'm telling you, I AM LONELY!', there's good news – loneliness is impermanent. It won't last forever. Feel your way through it – don't run from it or crack out the yellow paint, but know that it is a moving, organic thing that is ever-changing. That's why there are good days and bad days, and unexpected moments of sorrow over restaurants.

While it's comforting to know that loneliness passes, we also have to remember that having people around us to entertain us and make us feel loved is impermanent. That is reality, and once we expect that it's constantly changing, life is a lot easier.

Admitting to loneliness is embarrassing, which makes it even more isolating. From the time we venture out into the world as young children, we're taught the importance of playing nicely and sharing so that other children will like us and play with us – so we'll end up with lots of friends and won't be *lonely*. You see, grown-ups see loneliness as a terrible affliction. 'I actually think she's lonely,' my mum would whisper about a single friend, as though it was the most undignified condition from which to suffer. I always thought there was a suggestion of fault, like loneliness was a result of character flaws or lack of effort. One thing was for sure: loneliness was a pathetic state of being.

Mum worried terribly about two women in particular who couldn't snare a man for the life of them. 'I just think they must be so lonely!' she used to say. These women 'flatted' together, as they used to say in the olden days of the 1970s. As time went by, they travelled together, spent Christmas together, and eventually bought a house together. It turns out that they've been far from lonely. They're a couple to this day. They decided not to make it a 'thing' in their conservative, country Queensland community and kept it under wraps until a few years ago. This story serves to remind us that we never really know what's going on behind closed doors. Our perceptions about who's lonely and who isn't can be very wide of the mark.

Case in point, Mum will now admit that some of the loneliest times of her life were during the period when she and my father worked together for twelve hours a day, running a small shop. It was meant to be a great family endeavour and to appease Mum, who complained that my father was never around, but it was destined to be remembered as the only time in their forty-plus years of marriage that she ever seriously decided she wanted out. I guess she was pining for the guy she thought my father would be under those circumstances, whom he decidedly was not. In a visual and symbolic display of her unhappiness, Mum stopped speaking to my father and removed her wedding ring. He didn't notice either action, which must have made her feel very lonely indeed.

Thankfully, my parents sold the shop and went back to separate working lives, giving them something to talk about each night, and hostilities – and loneliness – ceased almost immediately.

Even when we are wanted by lots of other people, we can feel loneliness because *one* person no longer wants us. For that reason I think my friend from the start of this chapter, who's sad there's no-one to tell about his son's monkey bar achievements, is actually lonely. As a single dad to a couple of kids, he's definitely never alone!

Even though he's very angry with his ex-wife, he still pines for her, or at least for the *her* he dreams she could be. His delusion of her. The two of us often talk about our break-ups, and whenever we do he eventually sighs and says, 'It could've been so great.'

Like many of us, my friend waited for a very long time in the hope that his wife would 'come good'. We wait and wait for our partners to snap out of it, wake up to themselves, or whatever other euphemism we use to describe the complete personality change we're praying for. Hopefully we eventually realise it's not going to happen. But it's really hard to kill off that hope completely. It flares up every now and then and we feel lonely for them (or the *them* we wish existed).

I've fallen prey to the same kind of loneliness, a pining for someone who doesn't exist. I combat it by thinking about the truth.

I found the source of the problem, sure enough, and frustratingly it was identified right back at the beginning of our relationship by another psychologist – bloody know-it-alls!

It took me a very long time to be able to see it as clearly as that. For years I felt enslaved by it; I couldn't stand being with Adrian, but I also couldn't stand being away from him. I wanted to break free of the marriage, but I couldn't drag myself away. I thought it would drive me mad! Finally I realised I had to do what we always have to do to overcome negative emotions: drill down deep and be honest about what I was feeling and why.

When Adrian and I first met, I was seeing a psychologist for depression and anxiety. As more and more of our sessions were taken up with talk of my new boyfriend, the psych made the observation that I seemed to be idealising this guy a bit. He said he thought I was 'putting him on a pedestal' that Adrian could never really live up to. I brushed this comment off and forgot about it for many years – until I committed myself to dealing with my real feelings for Adrian as our marriage was falling apart.

That was when I realised there'd been a third party in our relationship from day one. I call him 'imaginary Adrian'. Imaginary Adrian looks like real Adrian and his voice sounds the same, but just about everything else about them is worlds apart.

They weren't so different in the old days, the two Adrians, but as we grew older, real Adrian bore less and less resemblance to imaginary Adrian. I became annoyed and impatient with real Adrian as he transformed into what I thought of as a 'grumpy old fusspot'. Imaginary Adrian was still youthful and carefree. He loved spontaneity and laughed all the time, while real Adrian grumbled about the slightest change in plans and hated leaving the house. Imaginary Adrian was still passionately in love with me, while real Adrian winced at the sound of my voice and slept in a separate bed.

God, I'm feeling lonely for imaginary Adrian now. What a spunk he is!

Of course he's my ultimate man: I invented him. But, alas, he isn't coming for me – not now, not ever. My loneliness for imaginary Adrian is silly. It hurts like hell, but I know it's silly. I have to make myself face that truth several times a day sometimes, to make the loneliness for him go away. I have to stop whatever I'm doing, take a deep breath, remind myself what's real and what isn't, and get on with my real life.

I have to reconnect with the positives of my break-up. There is excitement there, for my independence, and there's a sort of relief to accepting I'm on my own, where there used to be anger and frustration at not feeling supported.

I'm inspired by myself (!), the strength I've mustered, and at the lack of fear I now have about keeping myself and the kids not just alive, but prosperous and happy. I really believe I can do that on my own now, and that's a wonderful, liberating feeling.

The first time I faced up to my loneliness for imaginary Adrian wasn't so inspiring; it was devastating. I pushed it way down to the bottom of the laundry basket of my soul, and tried to forget what I'd discovered. Eventually, though, I was in so much pain and I'd waited and begged Adrian for so long to make it stop, without success, I knew I had to dig out the truth again and keep looking at it until it stopped hurting.

As with most things, actually doing it wasn't as bad as anticipating it. It didn't take too long – six months maybe – of forcing myself to see Adrian as he actually is and then conjuring up my imaginary Adrian and playing spot the difference. The more often I did it, the less painful it was, and the less shocked I was by real Adrian.

When I wasn't as annoyed by real Adrian, I was able to come to a more logical acceptance of our incompatibility. Dexter from *Perfect Match* popped into my head often: I'd hear his robot voice say, 'With a compatibility score of zero, Adrian is not your perfect match!'

I used to tell Adrian it all could've been so great, if only he hadn't ruined it. But now I've stopped thinking like that – partly because I stopped myself thinking about how great it once was.

I found myself increasingly able to think about breaking up without leaping to some hysterical extreme. I was able to lie in bed at night and consider the inevitability of it all without sobbing quietly into my pillow and blaming Adrian for everything. My old reflex was to constrict every muscle in my body at the thought of separating, but increasingly I could not only think about separating from Adrian, but think past it, to what a life without him might look like and feel like. I thought about the person I might be if I wasn't so worried about the future of my marriage and so upset about it all the time. Who would I be if I wasn't sitting in my car at the beach crying several times a week? If I wasn't trying to figure out how to make Adrian change?

The fact was, Adrian was who he was right then, and if I couldn't love him for that, then I had no business being with him. My constant haranguing and browbeating was terribly unfair to him. He deserved to be able to be himself in his own home without having someone constantly telling him to change. Everybody deserves that, whether it suits our fantasies or not.

As you've no doubt noticed, I'm a fan of counselling. I've seen psychiatrists and psychologists intermittently throughout my adult life and have found them a great source of comfort and help with self-realisation. The fact that modern psychology and Buddhist philosophy work so harmoniously together means that I usually find it pretty easy to engage with a counsellor and I tend to get a lot out of just a few sessions. These guys are professionals. They know how to help you feel better, so give them a shot if you're unable to feel better by yourself at the moment. Your GP can help you get started.

I also attend my Dharma centre regularly for teachings from the monks, which helps me keep my head together. And I sometimes visit them one-on-one if I have a particular issue that's worrying me. We have a name for this in our family: 'running it past the robes'.

I've never run something by the robes and not come away feeling better for it, and, similarly, I've never regretted seeking counselling, although I have had to shop around a little. Don't hesitate to try a new counsellor if you feel like you don't click with the first one you see.

You may well have some friends or family members who'd be good for a yarn. You could ask them. But be mindful of their limitations. Another friend of mine confided in her father about her worries, and he promptly burst into tears. You don't need that! Look at your friends and family as they really are, not as you'd like them to be – they may or may not be the right support network for you right now.

When it comes to tackling loneliness, there are a number of common mistakes we make that send us scurrying back into our lonely little holes. Engage your brain before you hit someone up for a chat.

DON'T:

- talk to your parents if you always come away afterwards feeling stupid and judged, or if you'll end up consoling *them*

- talk to your frenemy who always makes everything about herself and will gossip about you

- call your friend who's married with four kids under five, at dinner time, and expect her to be able to focus on you

- sniff around an old ex (It was just as bad, remember?)

- get drunk and talk to randoms. Anyone who'll sit and listen to a stranger's troubles is working an angle. Do you really want to wake up next to them? Sober??

TRY THIS INSTEAD

- Meditate on Emptiness and Impermanence. Adopt more positive language around being alone. If you remind yourself often enough that aloneness is a positive and a luxury, your mind will start to think differently.

- Concentrate on the positive aspects of the life you're building. It may help to write these down. Or make a vision board, if that's your bag. Cut out pictures that represent your goals and make a collage to stick on a wall. Take a deep breath and look at it, often.

- Reach out respectfully (i.e. not hysterically crying at dinner time) to trustworthy friends and family. Make a date to visit them or meet for coffee, and let them know you're feeling a bit lonely. That'll help them to know what you need from them. I recently visited a friend while she packed for a holiday. It's not the kind of thing you'd usually invite a friend over to witness, but she knew I was feeling a bit lonely for my kids while they were with their dad, and it was a perfect, low-key catch-up. An elderly Hungarian widow in our street sometimes comes down to weed a little garden outside my kitchen window. He speaks very little English, and I speak no Hungarian, but the hustle and bustle of our place seems to cheer him up quite a bit. I guess it helps him feel connected.

- Get out and do things you like to do. That's how you'll meet people who like to do them too, and you'll have something to talk about.

- Try volunteering. It's great for shy people, because you don't have to search for opening lines or try to find the courage to approach someone. You'll have to talk about what you're doing. Plus, the people you meet will be volunteers, so they're probably lovely.

- See your GP if you feel you're not getting anywhere. You'll be amazed at how ready and able they are to help with loneliness.

KEY POINTS

- Aloneness does not necessarily equal loneliness.

- Break-ups create a tug of war between wisdom and fear.

- It can be embarrassing to admit we feel lonely, whereas aloneness can suggest victimhood and abandonment. It may be easier to admit to feeling 'alone', but it's harder to work on. We need to focus on who we are and where we're going, not what's been done to us in the past (which we have no control over).

- By definition, aloneness means we are not in a fantasy-driven relationship. That is a very healthy place to be.

- Being alone is beneficial because it gives us time to work on ourselves.

- Aloneness gives us more influence over our own arising.

- If your fear is based on low self-esteem, then work on your self-esteem. Focus on the cause rather than the symptom.

- Introspection can help quiet self-criticism.

- Aloneness is easier and more peaceful than living with someone you fight with constantly.

- It's there anyway, but you can begin to heal it by facing it. You are built to heal.

- Buddhism requires self-reflection. It gets easier with practice.

- Reading about Buddhism is a great way to ease in to introspection.

- Aloneness will help you process your broken relationship and other painful experiences.

- Aloneness will help you leave the past in the past.

- Learning to be alone confidently means never clinging to anyone again. It gives you freedom.

- 'Loneliness is poverty of the self. Solitude is richness of the self.'

- Loneliness occurs when we forget our interconnectedness.

- Don't let others convince you you're lonely if you're not.

- Remember Impermanence! Loneliness is impermanent, but so is company. No-one else can rid you of loneliness. At best others can distract you for a time.

- Professional counselling can work beautifully alongside Buddhist philosophy. Seek out both if you are struggling alone.

- Reach out to friends and family, but respectfully and realistically. No randoms!

SELF-REFLECTION

- Which is winning in your life: wisdom or fear?

- Have you been employing dangerous techniques to avoid aloneness?

- Are you afraid of being alone? Why?

- Is it the depth of your emotion that scares you?

- Are you lonely for a fantasy you created yourself?

- Connect with the positives of your break-up. Who are you without the fighting for and about that relationship?

- Remember Emptiness! What unhelpful labels are you using to reinforce the idea that you are lonely?

8

Wisdom and Compassion

Although it may seem an unlikely combination of concepts, to Buddhists, wisdom and compassion go together like Netflix and chill. They probably also seem a bit peripheral when we're supposed to be talking about break-ups but, believe me, they're both crucial to the healing process.

Wisdom is always needed when navigating a break-up – but especially for anyone attempting to leave an abusive relationship. Any break-up is confusing. It's impossible to know if we're doing the right thing, because in reality there is no right thing. There are only actions and reactions, cause and effect. Whatever you do will set other things in motion and as we have no way of knowing what those things will be. But some outcomes are more likely than others.

Remaining in an abusive relationship will probably bring about negative outcomes, but all too often leaving such a relationship can seem more daunting than staying in it. Statistically, the most dangerous time for a woman in a violent relationship is just after she's left it, so while the Buddhist perspective is to avoid future thinking, we must temper that with wisdom. Do not be naive about the fact that break-ups often take planning – and if you think you are in a dangerous situation, get all the support you can before you embark on leaving.

The compassion part is more challenging because it can be counterintuitive to our modern Western way of thinking. We are much more likely to vow not to forgive a former partner than to cultivate compassion for them. We may even have supporters who feel it's their duty to prevent us from doing so. But cultivating compassion for someone who's hurt you is enormously beneficial to your own healing and future happiness. It's the opposite of holding on to anger and developing bitterness, but it doesn't mean exposing yourself to danger and manipulation again. Compassion can be cultivated from afar. In fact it is often easier to do that way. It's not about what the object of your compassion knows or thinks about it, it's about your peacefulness.

All too often in modern Western society, compassion is characterised as intrinsically lacking in wisdom. People who prioritise compassion are labelled 'bleeding hearts' or 'loony lefties' by rich old white guys on talkback radio. Those guys will tell you that wisdom comes from ignoring compassion in favour of more worldly concerns like money and power. They're either ignorant fools or lying for cash, but we'll come back to them when we discuss Karma.

I'll leave it to the boss to do what he does best, which is to explain potentially confusing concepts in simple English. In *The Essence of the Heart Sutra*, His Holiness the Dalai Lama wrote, 'According to Buddhism, compassion is an aspiration, a state of mind, wanting others to be free from suffering. It's not passive – it's not empathy alone – but rather an empathetic altruism that actively strives to free others from suffering. Genuine compassion must have both wisdom and loving kindness. That is to say, one must understand the nature of the suffering from which we wish to free others (this is wisdom), and one must experience deep intimacy and empathy with other sentient beings (this is loving kindness).'

From a Buddhist perspective, we're expected not only to be unselfishly concerned about others, but to make an effort to help and alleviate their suffering. Don't just think about it and feel pity for people, get off your butt and do something!

His Holiness is passionate about altruism and has spoken about its importance at some point during every teaching I've attended, no matter what the topic. As he told Oprah, 'Altruism is the best source of happiness.'

I've found that statement to be so true. Altruism made me feel happiness like I'd never known. It's like a wonder drug! I'm an active person by nature – not in a Zumba kind of way, but in a keeping busy kind of way – so committing myself to

ALTRUISM the principle or practice of unselfish concern for or devotion to others (opposite of egotism)

compassion and altruism was great for helping me feel like a real Buddhist. I took every opportunity to practise, from leaping out of my car to assist old ladies with their groceries to volunteering at Dharma events interstate, and it helped me to integrate other teachings and ideas into my day. I loved altruism sick!

Unfortunately I forgot about the wisdom bit.

There's an old theosophical saying: when the student is ready, the teacher appears. And my teacher came in the form of an angelic-looking little white fluffball of a dog called BJ (which stood for Bobby Junior, because he looked like the twin of my other dog, Bobby).

About a month after we adopted him, BJ leapt up to a height roughly three times his own to bite a delivery man in the groin. It was a complete shock to us, because he'd been perfectly behaved around the house. It was a shock to the bloke too, I can tell you. I apologised profusely and he kindly let it go, but in the years that followed BJ went from bad to worse. Eventually he bit every member of our extended family and several neighbours after digging his way out of our yard.

I spent thousands on specialised training with various companies across two states, to no avail. One day another neighbour rang the bell to say BJ had dug out again and attacked him in his own driveway. Talk about compassion! This guy was a compassionate master. He said to me, 'I'm sorry, love, I understand what you're trying to do, but you've got no choice. Either you deal with this dog, or the council will. I'm not going to complain about him but I can't speak for the next person.'

BJ was euthanised by the vet at our local shelter after months of their intensive training had failed to help him. He was cremated and his remains were returned to me in a small timber box with an engraved metal plate on the top that simply said 'BJ'. I was absolutely devastated, and my children still think he's living on a farm with lots of other dogs, so please don't bring it up if you run into them.

I was ashamed to talk about it, but my Catholic upbringing made me feel like I needed to confess what I'd done and take my punishment. I needed to run it past the robes.

I drove out to Paraparap in rural Victoria to visit my Tibetan teacher, Geshe Sonam, at the Drol Kar Buddhist Centre. He is something of a Buddhist prodigy, having become a Geshe, which is like a professor of Buddhism, at a very young age. He has full authority to deal with the likes of me! (Not that monks are big ones for punishment of course, but being raised Catholic, I was expecting some kind of penance would need serving.)

He sat attentively, listening as I told him the whole sad story, and then he smiled gently.

'Oh, this is not your fault,' he said. 'You tried your best for many years, but he was hurting people.'

'But I killed him,' I spluttered, wondering if he'd missed that detail somehow.

'Mmm,' he said thoughtfully, 'when I have mouse in ceiling, I kill mouse!'

'You kill things?' I asked, with eyes like saucers.

'Yes!' he exclaimed, 'of course! One mouse means many mice. Many mice make people sick and ruin house with chewing. Might cause fire. I must protect people and house. I must kill mice.'

He went on: 'This small dog, he was accumulating very much bad Karma by biting. You have ended that. You were accumulating bad Karma by keeping dog who hurt others. You have ended that. Dog can move on to next life, hopefully better. So, that's it!'

'That's it?' I asked.

'That's it!' he said with a wave of his hand as if to say, 'bring me a tough one next time, will you?'

'No more compassion without wisdom, okay?' said Geshe Sonam as I climbed into my car to leave. 'Google it.'

I did google it, and it changed the way I saw lots of things in my life, including my marriage. Buddha believed it's crucial that we develop compassion for people we feel have hurt us, and even for people who want to hurt us. So with that in mind, I'm going to ask you to do something that may seem crazy, pathetic and even unsafe at first, but bear with me: I'm going to ask you to wisely cultivate compassion for your ex.

You may feel as though you hate that person, and they may have done some horrible things to you, but remember what holding on to anger is like.

The opposite of holding on to anger and hating someone is cultivating compassion for them. Ultimately, we want to be able to think about everyone in terms of their struggle, and genuinely wish for every person to be free from suffering, even those who've hurt us. In fact, I'd be inclined to say *especially* those who've hurt us, because that compassion will be of great benefit to us in healing from that hurt.

I know my ex-husband very well, and I know what his struggles are. I've felt very hurt, angry and disappointed by his actions and words over the years, but I can overcome those feelings now by thinking about his struggles (mostly because he's not here annoying me now!).

In the moment, it's really difficult, I know. If you're unlucky enough to have an ex who actually wants to keep upsetting you, you have a much harder task before you. The benefits will be greater though, because the confidence you reap by fending them off with the power of your own emotional discipline will blow both of your minds. It will change everything.

Don't forget the wisdom bit though! Don't put yourself in a vulnerable or dangerous position. Your ex doesn't even need to know you're trying to feel compassion for them. It's all about you and your head, and it has nothing to do with accepting or condoning poor behaviour.

I asked His Holiness once how he manages to maintain compassion for China, after almost seventy years of brutal oppression and the cultural genocide of Tibetan people. He told me that first and foremost he feels compassion for the Chinese people, who also suffer. Even the government officials who uphold the policies are suffering, he said, but he was at pains to point out that compassion does not mean weakness. 'We should not allow ourselves to be victimised in the name of compassion.' That, again, is where wisdom comes into play.

Let's look at some ways we can wisely cultivate compassion in our lives.

- Try to think of your ex-partner's conduct as coming from inside them rather than penetrating into you. So it's really just theirs, you see? It's not hurting you. Basically, I'm asking you to remove your emotions and judgements from the situation. Just think about what might be behind that other person's actions as though you're studying a specimen, and not someone you once loved.

- Don't try to solve the issues, even in your own mind. Don't let yourself get caught up in disappointment about the failure of the other person to work on themselves. No emotions, no judgements, just observation.

- Don't assign blame. His mother may have made a lot of mistakes, but you're going to have to find compassion for her too!

- Remind yourself that this is not your problem, but theirs, and without them working on it, it can't be resolved. Compassion means wanting others' problems to dissipate, but not jumping in and trying to solve them yourself. You can be supportive if it's wise to be so, but you can't do someone else's work for them.

- No-one is born bad or good. We're all the product of our dependent arising, so there is a cause for all of our suffering. What is your ex-partner attached to?

This last one is a potential minefield. There may be a possibility that you can help your ex-partner by drawing their attention to the idea of Attachment. If you feel it's wise to do so, try it, but please exercise caution and remember: this is not about changing your ex!

With every word I write I'm aware that some readers will have experienced family violence prior to and possibly after their break-up. We know that the period immediately after leaving a violent relationship is a very dangerous time. People who feel the need to control their partners and families can freak right out when their victims assert themselves and leave. Perpetrators can act out unpredictably, and I would urge you not to take any chances in this regard.

If your ex-partner is attached to the idea that you are their property, then all the compassion in the world isn't going to help you find peace unless you prioritise your safety and privacy. Compassion is not about weakness, remember? It's not about accepting victimisation. Don't let anyone tell you that offering chance after chance and accepting apology after apology is compassion. It is actions, not words, that define reality. If your ex-partner's actions are consistently disrespectful and/or frightening, then you definitely need to practise compassion for them from afar. We can do that in the same way we can learn from them without having to subject ourselves to their 'lessons' over and over again.

Self-compassion has to come first. Lama Yeshe (a very high Lama) simply said, 'Be gentle first with yourself if you wish to be gentle with others.'

Some people feel guilty about being nice to themselves, but self-compassion has nothing to do with self-indulgence or selfishness. I have an old friend who's been a heroin addict for about thirty years now. I've never met a more selfish person. He lies and steals from people who offer him kindness all the time – in fact, he's famous for it. Whenever a new friend of his appeals to one of his old friends for help with such a matter, we can't help but laugh. How can a man so well known for his dishonesty still manage to con people?

'Can you ask him about the fifty bucks I gave him for that book he never posted?' a couple of us were asked recently.

'Oh sure thing!' my mate answered, chuckling, 'I'll grab back that hundred I loaned him in 1994 while I'm there!'

As charming and beloved as this rapscallion is, there's no doubt he feels no compassion for himself. In fact, I think it might be his complete lack of self-compassion that acts like a vacuum, sucking in compassion from those around him. I've never known anyone to love themselves less and be loved by others more. His oldest friends have learnt to mix wisdom with that compassion, and have long since stopped loaning him money. We may *give* him money from time to time, which is a very different thing.

We're all aware of his struggles, their causes and what he's attached to, he's well-aware himself, and yet the poor man is unable to feel compassion for himself. Hence the thirty-year hamster wheel of self-sabotage.

This is how I cultivate compassion for myself.

- I think about the fact that I am one human being, born onto this planet of billions of people. I imagine myself as a baby surrounded by every other person on the planet.

- I remember that I am dealing with my own disturbing emotions and the consequences of the disturbing emotions of others around me.

- I broaden my focus to the natural world, which is full of its own forces that are oblivious to their effects on me. The rain and wind do their thing without waiting to see if I'll be okay with it, the solar system swings around itself without stopping to see if I'm dizzy, little dogs bite delivery guys without any consideration for how it'll affect my Karma, or theirs.

- I recognise that there's a lot going on, and I'm just one little person, trying to create a positive imprint on it all. I will fail, I'll forget, I'll do dumb stuff, and sometimes I'll act like a jerk, but I'll try, until I breathe my last breath, to be better.

Basically I cut myself some slack! Altruistically, I take care of my mind and body and seek opportunities for growth. Spiritual growth helps me to maintain self-compassion, which means I don't need to seek it out so much from other people. I'm more independent and useful to others. It's the old, 'put your own oxygen mask on first, before helping others with theirs' thing.

Perhaps thinking about life in this way can help you to feel compassion for others too. Think of that rude shop assistant as one little grain of rice in the nasi goreng of existence. It'll be hard to stay mad at her because she's a bit over it all.

KEY POINTS

- Compassion isn't passive pity; it's actively trying to help ourselves and others overcome suffering.

- 'Altruism is the true source of happiness.'

- Compassion without wisdom is undisciplined and potentially dangerous.

- We must cultivate compassion for people who've hurt us.

- Successfully cultivating compassion for our ex-partners will change everything.

- Don't forget wisdom!

- Compassion is not weakness or accepting victimisation.

- Compassion can be practised from afar. You don't need to be in contact with someone to feel compassion for them. Use wisdom to help you create safe boundaries.

- Self-compassion is crucial. It is not selfish. Everyone deserves self-compassion. It helps us achieve independence and become more useful to others.

9

Karma

A recent caller to my radio show gleefully told the story of how her husband had run off with her close friend and left her with nothing. That wasn't what she was gleeful about, obviously – the bit that made her happy was the closer: 'And now they're divorced and he's bankrupt, so I guess that's Karma.'

Karma's been a very exciting discovery for us Westerners, because unlike the Judeo-Christian idea of Judgement, which supposedly happens in some kind of grand courtroom in the clouds after death, Karma promises us the chance to witness other people's comeuppance in this life, which is a very fun thought.

I can understand that to the caller her former husband's troubles are delightful, but I don't know that it's exactly

Karma, at least not in the way she thinks it is. Karma is one of those concepts that's been widely mistranslated. While I'd like to believe that every aggressive driver who swerves around me on the freeway has some kind of annoying (though not life-threatening) traffic-related drama in store for them, which I'll have the pleasure of

KARMA the relationship between cause and effect

driving past, this sort of 'instant' Karma is actually considered very rare. So if you're keen to witness your ex-partner's downfall, you might be in for a long wait; in fact, you might never see it at all, so it's probably not the healthiest of obsessions. It's certainly not productive.

Resist the idea that you'll feel better when someone else get's what's coming to them, because you may never see it happen. Remove their success or failure as a factor from your life.

What Shakyamuni Buddha learnt during his enlightenment was that Karma, the relationship between cause and effect, is much bigger than moment-by-moment corrections and revenge. Karma stretches through eons and determines how, when and where we are born, and the conditions we'll face.

We Buddhists say that Karma is the answer to the question 'Why?' It's the reason why some people seem to breeze through life hurting people with no consequences, and why other people can't seem to catch a break. I use the word 'seem' very deliberately, because the truth is none of us really knows about anyone else's journey. Suicide can be the first sign a person gives the rest of the world that their inner life doesn't match their outer life, so it's simplistic to believe we know for sure how anyone else is travelling.

That said, though, I remember very clearly sitting in my first class about Karma, thinking about the patterns I'd observed in life since early childhood. I realised I'd been noticing an element of Karma at work.

Throughout my childhood I had a close friend whose mother was my mother's childhood friend. Our families were very close and we thought of them as cousins. I couldn't help but notice the fortuitous pattern of my friend's life. She was physically beautiful, athletically blessed and everything just seemed to work out for her: from the wealth she was born into to games of chance, she just couldn't lose! I always felt unlucky by comparison, not because she had better stuff, but because she seemed blessed in every scenario.

Now that we're adults, I'm able to see the ways in which I've been blessed with incredibly good fortune. There's been a definite pattern to the way my life has unfolded. It's taken a lot of blood, sweat and tears, but in the end I've pulled together more than my fair share of big dreams. From the long and winding road of my career to requiring IVF to fall pregnant, it's been neither quick nor easy, but I've always gotten there in the end. That, among other things, is my Karma.

Here's the idea: everything you do creates Karma, good or bad. This Karma attaches to you and brings consequences further down the road, potentially in another lifetime altogether. When things happen to us – good or bad – that's our Karma coming back, or *ripening* as we Buddhists like to say. Why do bad things happen to good people? Karma. Why do great things happen to rotten people? Karma. Why do some people get all the luck while others can't catch a break? Karma.

It's also why disciplining our destructive emotions is so important. They make us act badly, which creates negative Karma for us. Do I want to suffer in a future lifetime because I get mad at Adrian's bad driving? Hell no!

Karma is the cause of inequality on earth. It's the reason why one baby is born to Donald Trump, and another is born to an impoverished family living on a rubbish dump. That's neat, isn't it? I guess it means I deserve my good fortune and don't need to worry too much about less fortunate people because they deserve the life they're living, right? Ah, no. Woah there, Charlie! Let's apply some compassion and wisdom to this equation, and let's drop a dollop of Impermanence on top for good measure.

Even Karma is impermanent. We sort of work it off as we go. So let's say someone has a tragically short life: they've worked off a hefty chunk of bad Karma right there. Similarly, if someone lives a long, wonderful life, they're chewing through that stockpile of good Karma. For that reason, it's most important for the recipient of a fortunate life to focus on creating more good Karma for themselves. I hope those Kardashians are paying attention, because they're really chewing through it this time around!

The other thing about Karma is that it can ripen at any time. We may think we know the nature of this rebirth we're living now, but it can change direction in the blink of an eye. I think about that every time Michael Schumacher pops into my mind, which is often. I'm sure he and his family would have characterised his life very differently the day before his skiing accident. The accident changed everything, in an instant, and it'll never be the same again.

To be clear, I'm not suggesting Michael Schumacher *deserved* his terrible accident, any more than my Aunty Pat's wealthy neighbour *deserved* to win Powerball last year. Karma is neither punishment nor reward. It's the constant ebb and flow of cause and effect that in the end only serves to remind us of our interconnectedness and responsibility to each other.

The helplessness of a former physical and mental power-house like Schumacher reminds us all of our vulnerability. His continued survival gives his family the opportunity to care for him, which they do with staunch determination and dignity, thereby creating good Karma for themselves. His refusal to die and take that opportunity away from them creates good Karma for him too.

We are not slaves to our Karma. The circumstances of our birth are just the beginning of our lives. We know that some people feel crippled by adversity, while others are inspired by it, and that siblings raised in the same conditions can go on to live very different lives because of the choices they make. I know for sure they can have very different opinions about birthday parties!

Lives that appear to be brimming with the results of good Karma can actually look pretty scary when observed through the lens of Karma. I feel great sorrow and compassion for Donald Trump's sons, for example, when I see them posing beside beautiful African animals they've killed for fun. The karmic ramifications of that kind of conduct are terrifying. Those poor men are so ignorant to the truth of existence, I weep for them.

Similarly, I (try to) feel compassion for people who drum up hatred in our society. I once witnessed a conversation in which a shock jock joked with friends about using his radio show to incite hatred for Muslims. The 'joke' was that he doesn't believe a word he says, nor does he agree with the people he encourages to phone in to his show with ignorant, hateful opinions and inaccuracies. This man earns an enormous amount of money to present views that he doesn't personally believe in, and I don't think he's the only one, by a long shot. It's a disgrace and it makes me furious if I let it, but I try not to. I try to cultivate compassion for him and use every opportunity I have to express the views of compassion and humanitarianism that I truly believe in.

Jesus said, 'It is easier for a camel to pass through the eye of a needle than for a rich man to enter the Kingdom of God.' (Mark 10:25) He was urging compassion for fortunate people, because of the great temptations and distractions that hinder their spiritual growth. The opportunities for creating bad Karma seem to grow exponentially with the accumulation of financial wealth. Perhaps it's the fear of losing it that drives the selfishness we so often see in very wealthy people, or the belief that they live somehow beyond consequences. I suspect boredom also plays a part.

In the late '90s I supplemented my comedy by working as a receptionist in brothels around Melbourne. It was a great job for the most part, especially while I was working at the Transsexual Brothel in Port Melbourne. The sex workers there were a brilliant bunch who were always up for a laugh, not to mention a show tune, but the other thing that made it great was the clients. They were by and large wealthy, polite businessmen, aged from their forties through to their sixties. It was the only brothel I've ever known to be busier during the day than at night, as men wandered in with briefcases and expensive cashmere coats between meetings. There were no drunken louts or time-wasting window shoppers in this establishment.

The vast majority of these men identified as heterosexual. As one older transsexual worker put it to me, 'When they've done everything else there is to do in life, eventually they get around to us.'

I've never forgotten that, and it seems truer to me with every passing year I spend on this planet. The more we have, the more we seek. The more we've done, the more we want to do. Money allows us to push those boundaries, but it also distracts us from ourselves and our higher purpose.

Jesus also said, 'Blessed are the meek, for they shall inherit the Earth.' (Matthew 5:5) Here, he agrees with Buddha again, in teaching that unassuming humility and gentleness are the most helpful attributes when seeking spiritual prosperity and happiness.

Provided his parents are humble, spiritual people, we could consider the baby born on the rubbish tip the lucky one.

For the longest time, I believed and even told people that I had some kind of blockbuster-strength karmic good fortune in the area of relationships. How else could I explain the fact that I met my dream lover, Adrian, when I was so young? How miraculous it was that I'd never had to fool around with other boys and men, I'd never had my heart broken or learnt a harsh lesson in love. 'I guess I must've learnt everything I need to know about relationships in a past life,' I reasoned. 'It's just not something I have to deal with in this one.'

Talk about things turning around. Now I feel like I've done nothing *but* learn harsh lessons about relationships from Adrian. I found myself in my early forties with no under-standing of how break-ups work, and suddenly wishing I had had a bit more experience when I was younger. It might have give me the confidence to imagine a life after Adrian, instead of the brick wall I saw whenever I thought about it. Ahh, but that's my Karma, and all I can do is strap myself in and try to stay coherent enough to make positive decisions about it all.

It's Adrian's Karma too, lest we forget. We are sur-rounded by people with whom we have karmic history – we owe karmic debts to some of them, and some of them owe us. Relationships that come together quickly, with a sense of familiarity, like ours did, are full of half-fought battles and old scores to settle. The trick is to reach a conclusion somehow, so as to not have to pick up those battles again in another life.

Such was my attachment to Adrian that I'd have signed up to a million more lives by his side, but now I see the chal-lenges we've brought to each other and I sincerely hope we can settle our account and move on. We are still bound by our children, which means we have the rest of our lives to keep creating bad Karma around ourselves if we choose to. I think we're both onto it now though, and neither of us has the desire for anything but peace.

Hopefully we can create enough good Karma around our relationship that if we have to be born around each other again, I can come back as his cat. He's very, very kind to his cat.

On that subject, we can't talk about Karma without talking about cyclic existence, or reincarnation. No only does Karma determine the conditions into which we'll be born, but also the other beings we'll be born around. It doesn't promise we'll live with the same family over and over again, but rather that every one of us has been family at some time in the past and will be again in the future.

It's pretty wild when you think about it, and extremely beneficial when it comes to remembering our manners. His Holiness the Dalai Lama urges us to love every single being the way we love our own mother, because at some stage, they just might have been.

That is a very powerful concept to think about when you're out and about. Look at people and imagine they are related to you. Imagine they are family and you love them. Imagine it about a rude man beeping you at the servo, imagine it about a shy child in a window and imagine it about the person quietly cleaning up around you in the food court. Imagine it about your most hated enemy, and about the animals and insects all around you. Remember the reality of Emptiness, remove your labels, and cultivate equal love for everyone by believing they were once very closely related to you. Within that love will come the desire for freedom from suffering for all sentient beings and the determination to try to assist them in that – aka compassionate altruism. Engage wisdom to prevent yourself from hugging and kissing strangers who might not be as highly evolved as you are!

This process is called cultivating universal compassion for all sentient beings, and it is one of the most powerful and beneficial things you can do for your understanding of the true nature of things, and to create good Karma. It reminds us again of the interconnectedness of everything, of Impermanence and of the futility of Attachment.

KEY POINTS

- Don't hang your healing on someone else's failure. It may never happen.

- Karma is the answer to the question 'Why?'

- Instant Karma is unlikely. Karma stretches through eons of time and is bigger than moment-by-moment corrections and revenge.

- Karma is responsible for the patterns we see playing out in our lives.

- Everything we do creates Karma, good and bad, and will lead to consequences for us in the future – potentially in future lives.

- When things happen to us, that's our Karma ripening. Karma can ripen at any time!

- Karma is impermanent. We are working it off all the time, so we need to keep creating good Karma.

- We are not slaves to our Karma – we can make our own choices and create good Karma out of any conditions.

- The more fortunate our current life, the more important it is to create more good Karma. It can be harder to create good Karma during a fortunate life, because of all the distractions.

- There is a karmic element to all of our relationships.

- We must try to end karmic battles so as not to have to live through them again.

- We must try to remember that we are all related through Karma and cyclic existence.

- We must cultivate universal compassion for all sentient beings.

10

Rebuilding

Hopefully by now you know you have to rebuild yourself. I don't know about you, but my life felt like a pile of rubble after my break-up. On the positive side, I realised it was totally up to me how I put it all back together. You can't just let yourself be chiselled by the elements. You deserve so much more than that, and frankly the rest of us deserve more from you. We're all connected, remember?

The only person who can rebuild you is *you*. There's lots of assistance out there, but no-one can do the changing for you, and now is the time to get started. Beginning today, you have to think differently and speak to yourself differently. What we think, we become, so you have to think strong, positive thoughts now, like never before. It's time to activate your recovery.

Let's retrace the steps to recovery after a break-up:

- Approach life with Emptiness. Get rid of the old biases and labels about yourself, your ex, your life and your future. Look at the world as it actually is and check in with every person and element to see if they really are what you assume they are.

- What are you attached to? Love without attachment. Force yourself to create space in your relationships and stop grasping at people you love. Sit beside them, don't try to climb inside them!

- Be mindful. Stop thinking about the past and fretting about the future. Get with the here and now. Check in with yourself to see where your mind is. Recognise anxiety and depression as past and future thinking. Meditate to clear those distractions from your mind.

- Catch disturbing emotions before they lead to more problems. No good can come of letting your emotions run wild. You have to discipline yourself.

- Implement some wonderful changes in your life. Eat better, dance more, spend more time with friends, paint, write, run. Have fun!

- Learn to love being alone. Make time for it and use it as an opportunity to think through your life and process things. This is when you can tap into your true self and see how the rebuild is coming along.

- When loneliness strikes, drill down into it rather than run away from it. What is it really about? Loneliness is impermanent, like everything else, so it will end, but seek counselling if you are struggling. Reach out respectfully to friends and relatives. Don't wallow!

- Cultivate compassion for yourself and for others, even for your ex, and even for their new partner. Make sure you remember that wisdom must be applied to compassion. Compassion is the antidote to hate, and hate is a prison for you and no-one else. Don't overextend yourself or put yourself in harm's way. Compassion isn't about victimhood or letting people take advantage of us.

- Create good Karma for yourself whenever possible. When you catch yourself focusing on the connection you feel you've lost, remind yourself of your connectedness to all things. You have much to offer others, which is good to remember if you've suffered a rejection. Believe it or not, the fact you can read this book means you've had a very fortunate rebirth this time around (you're human and you're literate), so it's very important to create more good Karma to replace that which you're using up right now. Focusing on this lucky rebirth is a great way to combat the blues.

• Exercise. It always helps. It pumps those happy hormones around your body, fills your brain with oxygen and makes you feel like you're respecting your body and yourself. Exercise helps me connect the physical and spiritual sides of myself and creates a more balanced outlook.

So, how do we implement all of that into a workable lifestyle. It seems like a lot of things to remember, right? No worries: Buddha thought of everything, including a system by which to implement the Dharma into our lives: it's called a daily practice.

The best thing about a daily practice is that you can adjust it to fit your lifestyle and circumstances. I once asked a doctor what the best form of exercise for weight loss was, and he answered, 'the one you'll stick to'. What a fantastic, realistic way of looking at it. A daily practice is the same. If you make it too involved and time-consuming, you might end up skipping it more often than not, before abandoning it all together.

Rather than thinking through the list of jobs, think about what you'd like to achieve from a spiritual perspective. Get into the habit of saying something to yourself along the lines of, 'Today I will do my best not to harm others but to be of benefit to them.'

I like to think of the practical implementation of the Dharma as a program. When I'm working the program – following the Dharma and incorporating it into my day-to-day life, checking in with books and teachings regularly to help keep me on track – life runs pretty smoothly. Actually, that's a bit misleading. What I should say is life runs like it always runs, but *I* run more smoothly within it when I'm working the program.

I find it easier when I create a structure for myself that turns into a habit. The structure can't be too hard or time-consuming because I just won't get around to it if that's the case.

In the next chapter, I run through some fundamentals of forming a Buddhist practice and describe my own daily practice. You can fiddle around with the formula and find what works for you – find a practice that you can stick with. Key things to include are: setting your intention for the day, meditation of some form, and reminding yourself of Buddhist principles. Actually, sometimes I read Buddhist books and attend teachings on top of my daily practice, but it's my main tool for keeping in touch with the Dharma and with my spiritual growth goals. It really does change the way I engage with the world, and it keeps me mindful of the ways in which I want to engage. I keeps me striving to do better and to cultivate more positive habits.

Developing a daily practice of some description will also remind you that you are embracing change. You're owning it and you're instigating it. You're actively contributing to your own arising and that's a very powerful feeling.

Think of the way athletes train for big events, and how actors prepare for big roles, working tenaciously and improving a little every day. That's the sort of journey you need to commit to. And luckily you'll find that everyone around you will help you practise and sharpen your skills. Who needs a Dharma coach when you've got kids, workmates, parents and an ex-partner to contend with?

Every incident in your life is an opportunity to practise. In fact, you might want to adopt that as a mantra: I did for a while. 'This is an opportunity to practice!' I used to say to myself as way of talking myself down from anger or frustration. Say it as many times as it takes for it to work!

My friend Osher Gunsberg of *The Bachelor* fame has a mantra of his own. His is, 'Of course!' He doesn't say it in an exasperated, lost-temper kind of way, but always with a chuckle. '*Of course* the traffic's terrible, it's Sydney!' he'll laugh instead of freaking out about running late, and he is one hell of happy, peaceful dude.

11

Prayers and Daily Practice

Given that Buddhists don't believe in a God, don't think of Buddha as God, and focus inward for answers and empowerment, it's very reasonable to ask, 'Well, who are they praying to then?' The answer to that most Buddhist prayers are more like meditations – reminders of how we wish to be. We pray in the that it will help us to behave according to the Buddha's teachings.

HANDS IN PRAYER POSITION AND BOWING

Buddhist monks can usually be seen with their hands together in what looks like a classic Christian prayer position, as demonstrated perfectly by this emoji: 🙏

Christians generally use this gesture as a sign that they're communicating with God; Buddhists use it as a way to acknowledge the presence of a Buddha. Buddhists believe it's possible for all of us to attain Buddhahood – that is, to become fully enlightened – so we should really put our hands together and bow respectfully to everyone! While I don't quite have the confidence to go the whole hog, I do bow my head a lot, especially when I meet someone new. To some people, I might look like a massive wanker when I do this, but I don't care. It's a good way to practise humility and keep my ego in check.

MANTRA CHANTING

To me, the sound of hundreds of monks chanting is the most soothing, spiritually profound sound I can think of. There are lots of examples you can check out on YouTube; there are even a few of His Holiness the Dalai Lama in full chant mode, which I think are particularly special.

The purpose of mantra chanting is self-improvement; repetition cements Buddha's teachings in our minds – just as we learnt our times tables by repeating them in primary school.

There are many different mantras with different purposes, and the various schools of Buddhism have different favourites, but the essential all-rounder is Om Mani Padme Hum:

Om   *Ma*   *Ni*   *Pad*   *Me*   *Hum*
(ohm) (mah) (nee) (pahd) (may) (hum)
(Note: the "u" in hum sounds like the "oo" in book)

Tibetans decorate everything with their translation of this mantra, as seen below, and it's a very popular tattoo in the West. I'm sure you can see why: it's rather lovely. It differs slightly from the original Sanskrit, because when Buddhism arrived in Tibet from India around the fifth century, the Tibetans found some of the words hard to pronounce, so they customised them. Tibetans pronounce it Om Mani Peme Hung. (In English, that translates phonetically as Ohm Marni Pemy Hoong.) Feel free to use either pronunciation. As with everything in Buddhism, perfection is not the goal or the purpose. Intention is everything. If you accidentally mispronounce this mantra a hundred times a day, but take it to your heart, it's no less beneficial.

You might be asking yourself: what exactly am I taking into my heart? Well, this phrase doesn't have a literal translation, but rather is said to embody the essence of Buddhist teaching, reinforcing the six central practices. Gen Rinpoche, the revered Tibetan monk who established New Zealand's first Buddhist centre in Dunedin in 1985, summed it up this way:

> When you say the first syllable Om it is blessed to help
> you achieve perfection in the practice of generosity,
> Ma helps perfect the practice of pure ethics, and Ni
> helps achieve perfection in the practice of tolerance
> and patience. Päd, the fourth syllable, helps to achieve
> perfection of perseverance, Me helps achieve perfection
> in the practice of concentration, and the final sixth syllable
> Hum helps achieve perfection in the practice of wisdom.

The classic string of 108 Buddhist beads is used to count mantra recitations. Grabbing your beads and chanting 100 (or so) Om Mani Padme Hums every day will help you relax your mind and refocus on how you want to move through the world. It's also a great way to get into meditation if you've got a bit longer.

FUN FACTS ABOUT MANTRAS

Although universal, this mantra is closely connected to Chenrezig, the Buddha of Compassion. I did mention there were lots of Buddhas, yeah? Tibetans believe Chenrezig has reincarnated as none other than His Holiness the Dalai Lama.

Traditionally, there are either 108 beads, or a divisor of that number, such as 27. There are many theories why, but my favourite is that it's in order to ensure you get a hundred mantras out for every revolution – they add an extra eight, assuming you'll miss a bead here or there.

Tibetans have been known to use beads fashioned out of yak bone in tiny skull shapes to assist the user in concentrating on life and death.

TAKING REFUGE

Taking refuge is the basic, fundamental act carried out by people who decide to practise Buddhism: it's what makes me a Buddhist – not just someone who draws philosophical inspiration from Buddhism. You can take part in a formal refuge ceremony, where a monk will perform certain rituals, but more important is the decision itself and the private declaration, which goes something like this:

> I go for refuge until I am enlightened
> To the Buddha, the Dharma and the Sangha.
> By my practice of giving and other perfections,
> May I become a Buddha to benefit all sentient beings.

There are many versions of this declaration, but they all have one thing in common: the idea of taking refuge in the 'three jewels' – the Buddha, the Dharma (Buddha's teachings) and the Sangha (the community of monks and nuns).

We Buddhists generally recite this prayer three times every morning.

ALTER SETTING

Setting up an alter as a focal point for practice is common in Buddhism. Tibetan people enjoy colour and elaborate design, so their alters tend to have a 'more is more' vibe, with flowers, food offerings, bowls of water, incense, photos of favourite monks and various ceremonial bits and pieces. Zen Buddhism is much more minimalist in every way, including altar preparation.; one Buddha statue, a pot plant and a stick on incense will do the job from a Zen perspective.

The truth is, you can make it up as you go along, as long as your intention is right. Do you want to have the grandest alter of anyone in your Buddhist gang, or do you find great peace and focus from tidying and preparing your altar every day?

In the past I had grand altars and spent time setting up and dismantling them every day in accordance with classic Tibetan rituals, but that, my friends, was before kids. Now my 'altar' sits atop a tall chest of drawers in my bedroom and is definitely more along the Zen lines. I dream of having a lovely dedicated space for Buddhist practice again, but this will have to do for now.

SETTING YOUR INTENTION

Setting intention is the process of being very clear with yourself about what you'd like to achieve in a particular period of time (such as the day ahead of you). It's not the same as goal setting; rather, you determine how you want to 'be' in the world.

I set my intention every day, out loud (whispered, because the kids are in bed with me). I say something like: 'My intention today is to be patient and compassionate, at all times mindful of the Dharma.'

DAILY PRACTICE

Putting together these various components into a daily practice is a very personal process. There's no-one right way, and you'll no doubt refine it for yourself as you go along, but here are the bare bones of my daily practice. I like to practise first thing in the morning, but I have to be at work at 5.30 a.m., so I need to keep it relatively short and sweet.

Upon waking I jump in the shower. Then I creep back into my bedroom (I have to creep because my children sleep there too) and prostrate three times before my Buddha statue. I used to do full protestations – I'd get down on my knees and stretch right out on the floor before getting up again – but this is impractical now, so I do the simper version. I put my hands into prayer position and raise them over my head until they're sitting on my crown. In this way, I remind myself that

I seek to purify bad Karma caused by actions of the body and aspire to all the good qualities of the Buddha's body. Then I bring my prayer hands down and hover them in front of my mouth and throat. This symbolises my desire to purify the bad Karma caused by my speech and my aspiration to all the good qualities of Buddha's speech. Then I bring my prayer hands down and hover them over my heart. In this way I express my hope for purification of bad Karma caused by my mind, and my aspiration to all the good qualities of Buddha's mind. (It's interesting that we in the West tend to differentiate between heart and mind, while Buddha taught that they are one in the same.) That makes one prostration; I do three in total.

Next I recite the Refuge Prayer three times, and recite this prayer, known as the Four Immeasurables:

May all sentient beings have happiness and the causes of happiness.
May all sentient beings be free from suffering and the causes of suffering.
May all sentient beings be inseparable from the happiness that is free from suffering.
May all sentient beings abide in equanimity, free from attachment for friends and hatred for enemies.

I like this prayer for two reasons: it reminds me of Buddhism's reverence for all living things, and I find the last line important. It reminds me not to play favourites when I'm interacting with people, and to give the same level of respect and friendliness to everyone.

After my prayers, I chant Om Mani Padme Hum 100 times, and set my intention for the day, and head off to work.

When I arrive at work, before getting out of my car and going upstairs, I meditate for five or ten minutes, depending on how the time's going.

So, to recap, my daily practice goes like this:

1. 3 × Prostrations
2. Refuge Prayer
3. The Four Immeasurables
4. Chant Om Mani Padme Hum × 100
5. Set my intention
6. Meditate

The versions of the prayers I've used here come from a book called *Essential Buddhist Prayers, An FPMV Prayer Book, Volume 1*. It includes lots of lovely prayers and practices and is available online.

12

Foundations of Buddhism

For those of you who'd like to look a bit further into Buddhist teachings, beyond your immediate break-up-related needs, I've included here a few fundamentals of Buddhist philosophy: the Four Noble Truths, and the Eightfold Path.

THE FOUR NOBLE TRUTHS

1. Existence is suffering

From the Buddhist perspective, anything unpleasant is referred to as suffering: from a broken leg to a noisy neighbour, a cold pie at the footy to a broken heart. Life is full of irritations, minor and major, and we tend to react to those irritations with negative emotions. We are very rarely in a state of unencumbered bliss, and if we are, we get bummed out when it (inevitably) ends.

Buddha said that the first step towards Enlightenment was to accept that life is suffering. Deal with it. You're not doing it wrong, or unlucky, or a victim of life, and it's not going to suddenly get totally easy and fun one day. You're just chasing things you desire, like the rest of us, thinking they'll bring you happiness, but they never do, not for long anyway. That = life!

2. There is a cause of suffering

Great news, right? If there's just one cause, then it can't be too difficult to eradicate. Well, according to Buddha, the cause of all suffering is our old pal *craving*. What do you think about that?

I always find it really interesting to try to trace my suffering back to craving. Sometimes when I'm in a funk I'll ask myself out loud: 'What am I craving?'

Sometimes it's a simple as a craving for food, or needing a toilet break or some fresh air, but sometimes it's much deeper than that, and much harder to label. Sometimes it's downright disturbing! I might find I'm craving acknowledgment, or praise, or respect. It's quite embarrassing when you realise you're grumpy because no-one seems to remember you came up with that great idea they all love. It's embarrassing to admit that you're feeling mopey because you weren't invited to participate in something, or weren't included on some industry list of cool kids on an obscure blog that about six people in the whole world will read. Take it from me, craving dumb stuff like that is very embarrassing, and when you realise that's what's really wrong with you, it's much easier to get over it.

3. There is an end to suffering

Hurrah!

4. The end of suffering is the Eightfold Path

You didn't think it would be easy, did you? Ending suffering is a massive task. We need to change our beliefs, learn new skills and evolve beyond our old habits. But if your old way of living keeps leading you back to suffering, why not give the Eightfold Path a go?

THE EIGHTFOLD PATH

The Eightfold Path is the ultimate checklist for getting your life in order. While I can't promise it'll eradicate your suffering entirely (that's up to you and how hard you work at it!), I can promise that making changes in these directions will help.

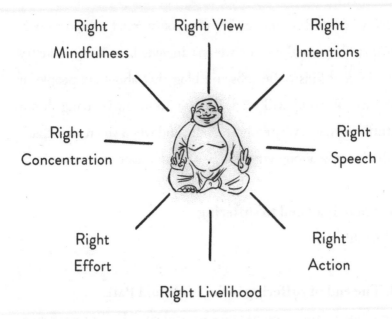

Right Mindfulness   Right View   Right Intentions

Right Concentration   Right Speech

Right Effort   Right Action

Right Livelihood

Right View: Seeing life as it really is.

Right Intentions: Always being motivated by generosity, love and compassion.

Right Speech: Truthful, respectful, positive communication.

Right Action: Following the five precepts, the basic code of ethical conduct taught by Buddha: don't steal; don't kill; don't lie; don't indulge in sexual misconduct; don't take drugs or other intoxicants.

Right Livelihood: Making a living that is not at the expense of others.

Right Effort: Having a good attitude and a balanced approach to life and work.

Right Mindfulness: Being aware of the moment you are in and being focused on that moment.

Right Concentration: Basically, pulling your head together, setting your intention, making up your mind and following through.

REFLECTION

It's time to ask yourself those questions again, the ones we looked at back in Chapter 2 on Emptiness. Let's see what, if anything has changed for you.

- Are you still in love with your ex, and would you want to reconcile?

- What was your part in the breakdown of the relationship?

- How does your ex make you feel? (Trick question alert!)

- What's the biggest thing you've lost in the break-up?

- Are there any advantages to the break-up?

- What does life look like now?

- Are you depressed and/or anxious? About what exactly?

Knowing the perfect answers to these questions and actually feeling them might still be two different things for you, but at least you have a program to help you work on them now.

I hope you will fight for your own peace and happiness.

You have brains in your head, you have feet in your shoes, you can steer yourself any direction you choose.

DR SEUSS